Selling Scripts
to
Hollywood

Selling Scripts
to
Hollywood

Katherine Atwell Herbert

ALLWORTH PRESS
NEW YORK

04   03   02   01   00   99   5   4   3   2

Published by Allworth Press
An imprint of Allworth Communications
10 East 23rd Street, New York, NY 10010

Cover design by Douglas Design Associates, New York, NY

Page composition/typography by Sharp Des!gns, Lansing, MI

ISBN: 1-58115-025-3

Library of Congress Catalog Card Number: 98-74533

Printed in Canada

For
Luella Irene Brown Atwell

The ideal mother who set
the standards for momhood

Contents

Introduction

"I always start writing with a clean piece of paper and a dirty mind," said Patrick Dennis, author of *Auntie Mame*. Other authors employ various methods. Some start with a clearly envisioned story and outline it. Others begin with an idea or an ending and go from there. And some, like Anthony Burgess, "start at the beginning, go to the end, then stop."

Any sort of writing, whether for the neighborhood newsletter or for next year's Academy Award winner, requires writhing and writing. You begin each day searching for ways to avoid the task until finally you surrender to your inner voice and take your seat at the keyboard.

If your dream is to get your stories on paper, you can't avoid the emotionally tortuous preamble. But you can find aids to keep your spirits up, your ego intact, and your goal before you. That is the purpose of this book.

We can all profit from improving our craft and our strategies to succeed. The purpose of this book is to offer suggestions, tips, and resources to meet those needs. Wrapped in and around that information is a little big-sisterly advice about surviving life as a writer.

There will probably be a spot or two in the book that you will find daunting. I could promote this book as an effortless method for writing and succeeding at the business of selling screenplays. But I refuse to insult your intelligence. Who's kidding who? If you believe those diet ads that promise a loss of thirty pounds in thirty days, or those health supplement stores that offer cures for every ailment, then you'll want to believe it's possible to write a screenplay and sell it inside a month. You won't find the formula for that feat in this book. Those promises carry in them the seeds of defeat. If you don't achieve their promises, you assume the worst and give up. I hope you find something much more useful and sustaining within the following pages.

CHAPTER ONE

So You've Decided to Write for Hollywood

SCREENPLAY: The form of writing that's overtaken the novel as a writer's preferred form of transport to the world of wealth, renown, and romance. And if the reality of it doesn't deliver the dream, at its very least, being able to tuck his own original screenplay under his arm puts the writer in the literate class in Hollywood, and there's something to be said for that distinction.

Membership in the writers' circle isn't the most glamorous or sought-after spot in the industry, but it is the one that engenders the most respect, outside the writer-director hyphenate class, which you may aspire to.

Achieving success in this area won't get your picture in *People* magazine. Journalists and (one assumes) readers of the popular press don't generally hunger for pictures of or information about Hollywood scriptwriters. Hiring a good p.r. person can help, hanging out at the right parties and charity functions helps, directing helps, and marrying a celebrity helps. But let's face it: as a writer, you'll probably never be as famous. Think about it. Would you really want to exchange your mind for a celebrity's physical endowments—both real and the recently discarded silicon? I'm thinking you wouldn't. So, let's accept our more subdued role and agree not to worry about it until Dow-Corning comes up with brain implants.

If you have something to say; if you have stories you want to tell; things you've got to expel from your mind so they'll leave you alone; then you're probably condemned to the life of a writer—with all of its exciting possibilities and its sometimes challenging realities.

Successful Attitudes

There seems to be at least a couple of attitudes, frames of mind, or assumptions possessed by many successful writers that propel them toward their goal of selling scripts and making money at it.

You really must believe that the stories you've got rattling around inside are aching to be told, to be shared with the world. Your motives aren't really pertinent, your overwhelming desire to get your stories aired is.

This need is akin to what motivates people who write letters to the editor or guest commentary. They harbor a tremendous need to express what they've got on their mind about a particular topic. They're convinced their views need to be heard so they can become part of the dialogue concerning current events. The driving need to write anything is based on the same desire. For whatever reason, you must want your offering to become part of the public's conversational, inspirational, intellectual, exposé, or pure entertainment currency.

When you're a beginner in any field of endeavor, sometimes it helps if you're blind to the competition. If you believe that your goal is achievable, you're more likely to give it a try. If you believe that you're going after this brass ring without fully realizing the great numbers who reach for the same prize, if you refuse to take seriously the fact that there is competition, you probably improve your odds of staying on track until you hit the tape. Because their emotional development is incomplete, young people are often only dimly aware of others' views, interests, and desires. Because of this, they are often unaware of the competition they face. They simply charge ahead. In Hollywood this is doubly advantageous. Not only are the immature heedless of their competitive situation, but Hollywood currently operates on the specious notion that youths automatically possess certain wisdom about the world, a wisdom that's referred to informally as hipness. Since many powers in Hollywood regard hipness as essential, the young have a head start. The tiniest knowledge of history exposes the youth-as-wise approach as running counter to all (successful) societies that preceded modern man, but, hey, that's Hollywood.

A third attitude that sustains struggling writers is the absolute belief that they are the best and only writers for the stories they have to tell. Further, it probably also helps if writers also believe (privately or not) that no one can write as well as they can.

Basic Requirements

If you are endowed with the foregoing attitudes, you will find that they take a beating day in and day out as you battle to achieve success in Hollywood. Mastering the more practical requirements of writing for the movies provides its own comfort and will help sustain your efforts when your 'tudes falter.

Writing requires literacy. When error-laden scripts arrive at studios they will be downgraded or rejected immediately. Who would hire a carpenter that didn't know how to use a hammer or saw? Sculpting stories requires proficiency in the science of using language accurately. Words are the writer's tools.

Research skills are also a valuable asset for writers. Even when a writer focuses only on what he or she knows intimately, there undoubtedly will arise a topic or two that will require research. From simple clarification, say, of how an ATM machine might jam or what your great-grandmother used for paper towels, to doing research on the fall of the Roman Empire or the latest discoveries about neutrinos, research will, at some point in your writing, become a necessity. The writers of *Armageddon* or *Deep Impact* needed, at a minimum, basic information on asteroids and comets. If you don't do the necessary research it will show. Your script might violate physical reality, violate the limits of the reality you've created, or insult the intelligence of your viewers.

There's another layering of skill that writers ought to possess to enhance their possibilities of success: a facility for the art of using language gracefully. Perhaps this particular ease can't be taught or learned. Maybe it qualifies as a natural gift or talent, but writers who possess or manage to develop a certain *sprachgefühl* and gracefulness with language have an advantage in the battle to gain recognition.

Practical Considerations

Screenplay and teleplay writing are specific forms of dramatic writing and follow certain conventions of story and format, topics covered later in this book. Understanding these conventions and adhering to format are essential if a writer is to succeed in Hollywood.

There are times when a script analyst reads a screenplay and notes that the work seems more suited to the novel form, or reads like a stage play, or perhaps the work feels like an elongated television sitcom.

Screenplay writing requires specific elements, such as a clearly definable protagonist. And although the great variety of movies playing in theaters worldwide would seem to counter this, nonetheless, commercially released movies, almost without exception, hit all the marks. Hopeful screenwriters, then, will educate themselves on the process, structure, character, and story development apparent in winning screenplays.

Know the Biz

To undertake the profession of screenwriting, not only do you need the proper attitudes, not only do you need the required basic writing skills and knowledge of the form, you also need an understanding of the field.

If your goal in life is to make a product that you're convinced is salable to every living thing (and with which you can make three fortunes), you've got a huge market. Once you decide that your product is screenplays, you must learn your market. Although you may think people of all ages, all over the world will love your script (movie), i.e., your product, it isn't that simple.

The market for your output is relatively small. Before cable, television writers and producers were well aware that they had three markets for their ideas and material: CBS, NBC, and ABC. They had to interest and intrigue buyers for the three networks or they didn't get their work aired. The addition of cable and over-the-air channels has broadened the market considerably, although many outlets have specific, narrower audiences than the big-three networks.

The feature film business goes through periods of expansion and contraction. In the mid to late 1980s several new companies came on the scene, thanks to Wall Street's interest in investing in entertainment. After several companies produced less-than-spectacular results, Wall Street turned to new areas of interest. Only a few of the companies begun at that time survive today, many in reduced form. While there are dozens and dozens of production companies, from one-man operations to large-scale organizations with studio deals, distributors for major Hollywood releases are limited.

It's like having two hundred companies producing shoes created by independent designers. The two hundred companies have to pick and choose carefully from among all the designs submitted to them, because, in the end, those companies have only a few distributors who can get the shoes they've developed into the stores. Ergo, in reality, your market is small.

And while there are hundreds of struggling independent film production companies around the country, without access to the major distributors in Los Angeles, the films they actually produce will have little if any chance of being seen by large numbers of people. With all the mini-indie companies around the country, movie-making seems like a healthy industry that offers scores of opportunities to writers. But, out of necessity, these minis spend most of their time raising money. And, too, these mini-minors are often run by independent writer-producers who have their own projects they want to film. Hence, they aren't particularly interested in developing other writers' work.

Small production companies doing business in Los Angeles usually have a better shot at success. They're in and around the business, they spend full-time at it, and they understand it's a business. They don't limit themselves to putting their own personal vision on screen.

There are companies other than the majors that will distribute your film. But if they agree to handle your work, don't invite your two hundred closest friends to the premier in your hometown. These distributors primarily represent foreign markets.

In short, because of the manner in which the business is organized, your work first has to pass muster with a small marketplace (production companies and/or distributors) before it can be enjoyed by a very large one—the world's movie lovers.

There is another important point that needs to be made about the film industry: As a writer you must understand that making movies is a commercial venture, just as is the company for which you presently work. Movies are made to entertain you and make shareholders smile.

If you think that the film business ought to make your film simply because it says something important, because it presents a moral view in an immoral world, because kids will like it, because it's near and dear to your heart, think again. But if your screenplay is also entertaining, well crafted, unique in some way, and presents the possibility that people might actually plunk down the cash to see it, then Hollywood may come knocking.

Other Helpful Traits to Acquire

What more do you need to be completely armed for this career choice? Let's reiterate some personal traits necessary to enable you to get where you want to be. You've probably read versions of most of these characteristics of success before, but they bear repeating.

Before you even pack up your word processor, you really are required to have the ability to write a script. Hollywood buyers aren't teachers, mentors, or people who have your best interests at heart. They won't send you notes telling you how very close you came to writing a good script and that if only you would change act three and the dialogue on page twenty-eight, your screenplay would be a splendid piece of work. If you're submitting scripts to professional production companies, they expect professional work. All your skills, craft, and abilities must already be honed. Imagine someone who just took an interest in automobiles presuming to fix your car and assuming you will be understanding about his lack of knowledge, skills, abilities, and familiarity with the trade. Ditto for your dentist. You get the idea.

Be prepared to stick to your career choice. With the extremely rare exception, first scripts almost never get bought or even given a second thought. Keep writing. If you get an agent interested in a work of yours, the first or second thing he will ask you (after you've swapped all the polite make-nice chat) is, "What are you working on now?" Agents want to know you're not a one-shot wonder, a lucky amateur, a dilettante, or a single story oddity. It may be that your script is well written but not really salable. They want to know if you've got other things they might be able to represent later. Most successful screenwriters have a drawerful of early efforts that were never sold. They may have served to get a door open. They may have simply been, unknown to the struggling writer at the time, practice.

Like good salesmen, writers have to sell themselves—all the time. This is true of every freelance writer (and every freelance anything). When you meet possible buyers, or people who know buyers, or people who know people . . . you have to convince them that you're a good, skillful, dependable writer who can do the work and knows the business. When you get the opportunity to pitch a project to an agent, a story executive, or a producer, you have to sell yourself. You have to present yourself attractively (that means brush your teeth before the meeting and put on deodorant), confidently, and professionally. The buyer has to be convinced that you know what you're doing, you can do it, you can do it within the framework required (time, budget constraints, etc.), you can successfully see the project to completion, and you won't cause an incredible number of problems.

You've got to act like a dog with a bone if you want to succeed in Hollywood. You must keep at it. You must keep trying. You must keep howling to get in the door. You have to dog it. The story staff at a studio where I worked was regularly treated to (or victimized by) a particular actor. He had met the head of production and the head of the studio on a previous shoot. They became "friends." Subsequently the actor often dropped by the office to say hello. He disturbed the office, and the bosses usually didn't have the time or inclination to see him, but he came anyway. He was either completely ignorant of good manners, or he knew better, but was so driven that he came anyway. He now has a comfortable career. He's appeared in dozens of films in substantial roles and currently is a leading character on a successful television series. He kept doggin' it. Is he where he wants to be? Maybe he still wants to be a romantic leading man, but meanwhile, he's working regularly, he's in an interesting series, he's making a very good living, and he has visibility—crucial for an actor. As a writer, you too have to dog it.

While you're writing those scripts and getting better and better at your craft, making your rounds and staying in touch with the people you should stay in touch with, making new contacts, and doggin' it, you'll also want to keep up and stay informed about what's going on in the business. This doesn't mean you should read the latest gossip about Leonardo or Keanu. It means maybe something you read in *Variety* or *Hollywood Reporter* might hold the possibility of an opportunity for you. You won't know about it if you don't keep yourself informed.

Hanging out with people who work in the industry is also an advantage. They all talk about their jobs, and through them you learn a little more about how the business works. Take some classes, and not just writing classes. This is the career choice you made; you need to give yourself as many advantages as you can. You need to know the nature of the jungle you're hewing a scythe through.

Finally, you have to learn to take rejection. There's a lot of it in all facets of the entertainment industry. Most of it isn't personal. Most people (other than salesmen) work in fairly routine jobs that don't include a lot of rejection. A few years back, as part of a company that downsized, I watched many employees who had worked for the employer ten or more years go through crippling anxiety, fear, and denial. They had apparently come to believe their jobs were essential. They also had no clue about job hunting. These people didn't understand the banal and impersonal nature of rejection. You must never let it dissuade you from pursuing your dream. You have to keep on the track you've chosen for yourself. Throw off the inevitable rebuffs and keep on going.

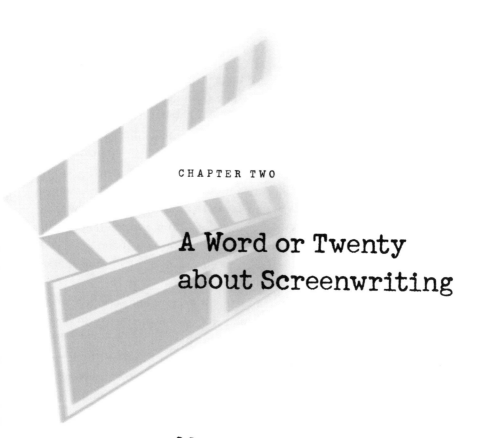

CHAPTER TWO

A Word or Twenty about Screenwriting

Maybe it's within the nature of American movies that people don't regard them with much respect. Cinema has always been the democratic art, generally eschewing any approach or topic deemed too abstruse for the masses; embracing any and all strata of talent, promotion, and moneymaking projects; and too often gauging its work to draw society's lowest common denominator.

Movies are a big, inclusive, profit-driven industry. As such, they've never inspired the regard that classical music or even theater has, although all three arts are dependent on attracting an audience and require a profitable box office to survive. (Albeit classical music and theater generally depend on donations and grants to maintain their offerings.) Further, screenwriting has never achieved the status that novel writing has enjoyed. It's only been in the past twenty years that screenwriting has become a first career choice for writers. Because stories of untried writers winning large studio contracts, of two-sentence idea pitches doing the same, continue to flow from Hollywood, it's no wonder everyone assumes that screenwriters have the ticket to big bucks land. To bank your future on that idea you've got rolling around in your head you hope will become the next hot action flick is probably a poor gamble, unless you have the ear of Spielberg or Ovitz. If you don't, then remember that although Hollywood delights in telling stories (through the ever-present, palpitating media outlets) of neophytes overcoming impossible odds, the truth is generally quite a different story.

If you give it a minute's thought you'll realize it is actually quite demeaning to the profession of writing that people think anyone can write a bestseller or a screenplay without any previous experience, without working at it, or without failing a few dozen times first. Does any professional worthy of the name appreciate it when untrained applicants assume they should start at the top? Writing is a skill that has to be developed and practiced. Very, very few writers are natural born geniuses—fewer than any publicity material would have you believe.

So if you're new or from the school that thinks writing scripts requires only a good idea and making a pitch, and you assume that real writing skill is of little importance, it's time for a reality check in the form of a brief consideration of the basic elements of the screenwriting trade. Screenwriting is a very specific kind of dramatic writing with its own conventions and requirements, actually, more requirements than novel writing.

Quickly Now, The Basics

Let's just say this up front: It's the writing, stupid. Nothing happens in Hollywood without the written word. Without scripts, there is no need for anything, repeat *anything* else. No lawyers to negotiate contracts, no actors to memorize lines, no directors, no lighting or art directors, no nothing!

And, pal, it's real writing. It's the ability to use the English language well, to understand and respect the language. It is what you use to form, shape, and refine your creations. You need a good, solid background and skill with language, specifically English. Beyond understanding the basic writer's tool, which is a need both novelists and screenwriters share, screenwriters also have other considerations.

Successful Hollywood screenwriting is about storytelling. There are other kinds of scriptwriting, for such things as educational films and art films, but the currency of Hollywood is the narrative, usually fiction, script. To write a good Hollywood script this must never be forgotten. Hence, you need to understand the principles of storytelling.

One simple way to do this is to think of the last joke you told. You set up the joke first. For example: When Mother Theresa died, she immediately went to heaven. When God heard she had arrived he called for her. There, we set up our story. The second part of most jokes is the complication. When Theresa gets to God's chamber he tells her he is overjoyed to see her. She, above all his earthly creatures, was ideal. She led an exemplary life, unequaled by practically anyone on earth, except maybe Albert Schweitzer. Theresa thanks him. God tells her that since she had been so pure in heart he would like to offer her anything, (our complications) anything at all, whatever she wants. Theresa replies that she is perfectly happy. "But there must be something you want to do, see, be," God persists. "No," Theresa says. "My life was completely fulfilled. I couldn't ask for anything more." God presses on, "Surely there's something, some secret desire that was never realized." "No," she replies, "Being in your presence is enough." "Oh, hell, Theresa," God says, "Cut the crap. There must be something you want." (We've set up this joke, developed it, and now we're ready for the payoff, the finale, the climax.) God looks hard at Theresa. She looks back at him and blinks. She swallows and says in her most humble voice, "Well, there is one thing." God says, "I knew it!" Theresa continues, "I'd really like to direct."

So there it is: the three-act structure.

Whole texts have been written explaining the script writing process, but that isn't the focus of this book, so we won't get into a detailed discussion of it. But, let's just do a quick review of the basics.

Three Acts Please, Over Easy

Ask anyone in Hollywood about screenwriting and they'll talk about the three-act structure. The three-act structure is a way of organizing your story. It's the way we've learned to watch movies over the past century. Yes, there's room for the unusual, for surprises, for twists, turns, for taking the audience where they least expect to go, but underneath it all, like a building's girders, the three-act structure provides the support and holds the story in place.

The three-act structure isn't new. Aristotle talked about it in *The Poetics*. Essentially, it follows a pattern similar to the previous joke. It's also flexible enough to accomodate other writing theories, such as the hero's journey.

In act one you set up your story. You clarify whom the story is about and locate the audience. Locating the audience means that by the end of this short act the audience will know what century and where on earth (or in the heavens) they are. Additionally, the audience needs to be located with regard to the type of place they are visiting, what the people are like, what mood and attitudes prevail. Think for a minute about *Blade Runner*. It is only a few minutes into the story that we know we are in a future rainy and neon-lit Los Angeles. We know what kind of transportation is used in this crowded dark world that is none too friendly and apparently gave up the ecological battle years ago.

By the end of act one, we know who our main character is, what he does, and the nature of his assignment, which he is forced into accepting. His acceptance is the inciting incident that launches the story. In as brief a way as possible, that's what act one is supposed to do. Watch *The Fugitive*. It too follows this pattern, as does *There's Something About Mary*, *The Mask of Zorro*, and *The Opposite of Sex*.

Act one is done once the audience identifies the main character and what he must do. The hero's task is referred to as the hero's journey, the quest, the problem to solve, or other variations of the same concept.

The audience is now prepped to go along on the journey with the hero/protagonist. That's where act two begins. But act two is trickier. The hero can't simply solve the problem; he has to encounter complications, setbacks, and an antagonist who wants the hero to fail. In fact, by the end of act two, usually the hero is ready to throw in the towel. He gives up, takes a breather, or appears to be defeated. This is the point at which either something happens to change the odds of the hero winning, the hero reaffirms his resolve (oftentimes consummating his relationship with the love interest), or a subordinate character urges the hero on. Then, just barely recovered from serious wounds, reenergized by the pleadings of a loved one, or pushed over the edge by the situation, the hero comes back and is ready to face down his opponents (the act two climax). This act is finished and act three is about to begin.

It is in this final act that the story line must be resolved. After a tremendous battle (even if that battle is simply an argument, as it is in *The Fabulous Baker Boys*), the hero must come face to face with the antagonist, (whoever or whatever that may be), do battle, and emerge victorious—the film's climax. The victory may be as low key as the hero's realizing that he can't solve all of the world's problems or that he has to accept certain unpleasant truths about himself and his life.

There's another way of regarding the three-act structure. Act one: get your hero in a tree; act two: throw rocks at him; act three: get him down. Act one and three are short, thirty pages or less, usually less. Act two with its complications, failures, subplots, and supporting players is long, perhaps sixty pages.

The catch to developing this three-act structure is that this story of yours has to be told primarily in pictures. Cinema tells stories through pictures. So while the novelist may leisurely paint the scene with words and let us in on everything the hero is feeling, thinking, and experiencing, in screenwriting this task must be completed using very brief stage directions and naturalistic dialogue. It is through the actions and speech of the characters that we must understand all their feelings and know their personalities.

The Premise Must Have Promise

There's another catch. The problem or quest or journey must be of enough importance that an audience will care. If the problem is frivolous or completely inane, the audience simply won't care. Even in comedies, the characters take their lives seriously and their quest must be serious and meaningful to them. Think of *It's a Mad, Mad, Mad, Mad World* in which the characters have a chance of finding a fortune. Wouldn't we all jump at that?

The protagonist in *The Fugitive* fights to clear his once good name and reputation by finding out who really killed his beloved wife. That's a big enough problem for us to get behind. In *There's Something About Mary*, the hero wants to be happily married, as is his best friend. He's tired of a meaningless existence, and he wants to find love. That's another quest that draws us in emotionally. Zorro wants to save his fellow Mexicans from the arrogant Spanish governor. Yet another worthy goal.

Your Character

Movies require a character that the audience can care for, root for, get interested in, and hope will prevail. Think of Kevin Costner's character in *A Perfect World*. He simply wasn't sympathetic enough for the audience to care about. There have been other movies in which ex-convicts involved us in their plight, but there was nothing in Costner's character that allowed the audience to sympathize or empathize. Hence, the film failed. Unattractive, despicable characters may be more interesting, or truthful, and allow you to feel your work avoids a formulaic approach. Maybe you're right. Nonetheless, write such characters at your peril. As a writer you can never forget that commercial movies are a popular art, just as are most bestselling novels, which follow similar patterns.

Characterization, then, is the writer's other primary concern. While the novelist can go on for pages detailing all we would ever want to know about a character, the scriptwriter is severely restricted once again. With only a few descriptive lines and only a few suggestions indicating how the character is feeling at any particular moment, the writer has to create a believable, consistent character who possesses a wholeness, a recognizable human persona.

There are always criticisms of the one-dimensional characters in screenplays. Some of this is inevitable. There usually isn't time to develop all of the characters to their fullest extent. However, the leading characters certainly must be well defined. That means they must have a past, interests, points of view, attitudes, and prejudices. They must make decisions based on their past experiences, and behave appropriately for the characteristics you've given them. Think of Richard Dreyfuss's character in *Jaws*. If the screenwriter had suddenly written a scene in which Dreyfuss's character was the soul of politeness and refinement, saying "yes sir" and "no sir" to the mayor or the police chief, he would have been out of character. It would signal that the writer didn't think through his personality before committing him to paper.

Sometimes on television you see the supporting characters on sitcoms behaving very differently from one episode to the next. The character is jimmied so the plot and humor will work. Even in as good a sitcom as *Seinfeld* there were episodes in which George's behavior varied from what we had come to expect from him.

Writing biographies of each of your primary characters is one of the best ways to get to know and to define them. Then, when particular action arises in the story, you'll know how your character would act in that specific situation.

There is a chicken-and-egg aspect to writing scripts. Most writers will tell you story arises from character. Conversely, many producers will tell you that you've first got to have a great tale to tell. Remember, your story idea has to be something producers, agents, and script analysts haven't read or seen a dozen times in the last couple of years. But also remember that the characters drive the telling of the story. It is their actions and their decisions that get them mired in the story's problem. But, it's also their personalities that will eventually get them out again.

In short, as a short ending to a very short discussion of scriptwriting, the greatest restriction facing writers is that they must tell an engaging story well with very little supportive text and not an extreme amount of dialogue. They must let the action tell the story. And they must do it all in under 120 pages.

CHAPTER THREE

You Don't Have
to Write Features

After my previous book was published, I began getting asked to speak at writers' conferences and workshops. Most of the writers or would-be writers or the merely curious who attended these workshops wanted to write full-length, big-screen screenplays.

However, there's more to script writing than the big screen. Shortly after I moved to Los Angeles I met with one of the biggest names in television writing. He had begun as a mystery writer and moved to television in the 1950s. He said that being a writer-producer of a television show was about the best that it got in Hollywood. He could write a script for the hour-long detective show, and it would be produced and aired in under a month. As a staff writer-producer, he was always part of the process and could see the material coming together. According to him, to write material, be a part of its creation, and see it aired on national TV a week or two later was little less than heaven on earth.

In feature films there are many situations in which a script, purchased or optioned, falls off-track, and the writer is thrown back to square one with his work. In features it can be years between the day the first word is committed to paper and the day the screen is ablaze with the story. If a screenplay survives all the vicissitudes of the development process, it will be, at the very least, upwards of two years before the prints are shipped to theaters around the country.

Other Markets for Your Work

Many writers, in their quest for big-screen success, forget that there are many places where they could employ their ability to tell stories with pictures. The world doesn't end with feature films.

In terms of money and renown, prime-time television (fiction) writing is the next best thing to features. And in many cases the money is better. Although television production companies always try to wring the cheapest contract out of every writer hired for staffs of sitcoms or hour-long shows, still, the money is good.

If a sitcom writer wants, in her heart, to write for the big screen (and who doesn't), she usually has to prove herself to feature producers. Producers want to know if the writer of thirty-minute episodes can write a story that will last 120 minutes. Of course, the advantages TV writers have are that they've proven they can write, they've been working in the business, and they have agents.

Crossing over from one medium to the other is getting more common. As more popular comic television shows are turned into movies—e.g., *Beavis and Butthead Do America*—while the show is still on the air, producers are less skeptical. Although, in many cases, the thin, sometimes one-joke plots should have been more carefully critiqued by the producers. The point is, the shows bring name value to the marquee, and if the producers can get the theater seats filled opening weekend, then they're usually pretty happy.

Dying Is Easy, Comedy Is Hard

There's a lot of pleasure and prestige in being a successful comedy writer. You don't need any ambitions beyond this to sleep well at night. The really good ones are not a common commodity in Hollywood, and experience in this area is highly valued. It's accepted in Hollywood that there are only a handful of individuals in town capable of running a network. There are only a couple of handfuls of people networks turn to to develop new sitcoms, and there're only a half-dozen handfuls of successful, proven comedy writers.

Television comedy writers face a difficult working situation that can be a killer for the inexperienced or uncertain. Writers have to come up with twenty-six minutes of comedy; include at least a couple of story lines; make it funny; make it fresh; write it so it fits the personalities of previously developed characters; write it under time constraints; accept criticism from the executive producer, the network, the actors, and everyone else down to the temp production assistant (P.A.); take notes after the first read; rewrite; do more rewrites during rehearsals; and so on until the cameras start rolling.

On the other hand, the writer can get a few of his points of view about any and every topic woven into the story if she so chooses. Remember episodes of *Murphy Brown* and *Designing Women*? There is little doubt where these writers stood on a variety of issues. And you don't even have to build an episode around a specific theme like, say, surrogate mothers. A minor character can voice your opinion, as long as you weave it into dialogue that's witty and works with the story. Imagine having a national audience for your opinions on abortion or the presidency or wing-walking centenarians. Imagine seeing your name on the credits of the show each week. Imagine a cushy paycheck every couple of weeks. And imagine working with a staff of people who are as bright, funny, quick-witted, and ambitious as you. That's scary. And I mean that in a good way.

And finally, writers on sitcoms can aspire to positions that carry more responsibility and prestige. Most producers of successful sitcoms began as writers and eventually formed their own companies. And if you get into a position where you *create* a successful show, then you're a god—a creative god who also takes big checks to the bank every time an episode or rerun of an episode is aired, even if you only write a few shows during the sitcom's three-plus year run.

How do you get into this work? Are you funny? No, I mean really funny? Do you think funny? Can you write? Following is a super-express course on sitcom writing.

Stories for half-hour sitcoms are different from features. They're written in a two-act structure. Act one, comprising the first fifteen minutes of the half hour, is basically the set-up for all the story lines. There are generally at least two story lines (called the A and B stories), although *Seinfeld* often had a story for each of the four major characters. In act one the writer has to set up all these stories and get the coming complications in place and foreshadowed. Act two is the punch line. (Sitcoms are a little like a question joke: you set it up and then you pay it off. You know question jokes: Why did the president . . . or, Why did the chicken . . .) The complications come to a climax and everything goes wrong, or if not wrong, different from what was intended. The finishing touch is the post-climax result of the misfired schemes.

Writers have to keep in mind that the characters they are writing for are already established. You can't write things that would be out of character for any of the sitcom's personalities just to make your joke or your entire script work. You really can't create characters or suddenly give one of the show's ongoing roles a different backstory than has already been established. You're limited to creating minor one-episode characters.

Another thing about comedy is that you really have to rack your brain for an idea the staff hasn't already done. Sure as you tell them you have a story about how the characters get stuck at a dairy farm, the story editor will reply that they did that plot line two years back. You had better watch the shows you want to write for—so you'll know before you write what stories have already been produced.

By watching the sitcom of your writing choice you'll also determine the established setting used on the show. Some sitcoms are quite confined and you, too, better place your story in those sets. Others are a little more liberal with the movement of characters. But remember, most of your scenes will have to take place in maybe three different locations for the entire half-hour. Most of *Roseanne* took place in the living room/kitchen of the family home and wherever Roseanne was working for that episode. Most of *The Drew Carey Show* takes place at his office, in his kitchen/living room, and the bar where he and his friends hang out. Don't try to create new locations for your spec script. Every addition costs money that the business affairs people will insist isn't available.

The format for sitcom scripts is different from the format used with feature films. You need to know what that format is before you submit your spec scripts. It will be taken as a sign of amateurism if your work is not completed properly. More about this is in chapter 7.

Breaking into television is as difficult as breaking into features. Maybe harder. The best thing to do is write spec scripts. Keep writing them. Look for an agent who specializes in television writers. If agents turn you down, keep trying until you get one. You have to keep writing new scripts for current shows. Having sample scripts for *My Three Sons* or *Family Matters* probably won't impress an agent or a sitcom producer.

Television sitcoms strive to be very much cutting edge. Styles, attitudes, and approaches change quite rapidly in television sitcom writing. You have to stay on top of it to succeed.

TV Can also Get Dramatic

Hour-long shows occupy a place midpoint between sitcoms and feature work. When you think of it, an hour-long show is really half a feature film.

The similarities to sitcoms include continuing characters, established sets, and a consistent routine or format. On *Law and Order* the first thirty minutes are consumed with arresting the person or people who the detectives have determined committed the crime that opened the show. The last half is devoted to the prosecuting attorneys and their efforts to make a case. As a spec writer, you won't want to mess with this format, just as you wouldn't have messed with the *Hill Street Blues* or *Murder, She Wrote* format.

You need to understand the unique approach to the established characters on the show that you wish to write for. *Law and Order* spends very little time on the personal lives of its characters. Things are hinted at, asked about, and referred to, but very little is seen on screen of the characters' personal lives.

On *Homicide* the situation is nearly the opposite. We see the characters interacting dramatically with each other. They disagree; they sometimes don't like each other; they don't trust each other; they grudgingly come to each other's aid, and so on. Their personal lives have an important effect on their behavior at work, but we don't always see these off-the-job scenes.

One of the differences between sitcoms and hour-longs is the locations. Hour-longs, shot like film, use many different locations in addition to their established or home sets, i.e., the station house of *Homicide* or *NYPD Blue* or the emergency room on *ER*.

Hour-longs are written in four acts, each running about fifteen minutes. The story arc is very much like feature films, with act two and three substituting for act two of a feature. It's just that the whole thing is shorter. Many sixty-minute scripts also include a prologue or a teaser of one-and-a-half to two-page length. This is aired before the opening commercials to get you involved. The format used for hour-longs is the same as features, with the exception that the acts are labeled.

There's Still More Gold in Other Venues

Commercial, established fiction television is very competitive, offers good pay, and can be very satisfying writing (whether you admit it or not). As the cable networks have added their own series, both sitcoms (animated and live-action) and hour-longs, the same information applies. The pay is not as good. The competition is also fierce, but there may be a few more doors that can be opened. Cable is a newer game and is generally more experimental and open to fresh ideas with regard to types of shows, topics, length, and practically everything else. The downside is they usually have less production money.

If you have experience writing news, you can always investigate the possibilities of writing for one of the many newsmagazines on TV. (The prospect of even more of these in the future is promising.) These programs also have staff writers and producers. But they do buy freelance pieces. Their material is, naturally, very topical and often slanted toward what they consider investigative reporting in which they uncover various types of scandals or misdeeds. They also include lifestyle pieces.

This isn't narrative writing. It is more closely allied with print journalism, although some of the pieces seen on these shows seem like fiction. Experience at a local television station or a newspaper, as well as an undergraduate degree in communications or television, would help your chances of entering this area.

If you have experience writing other types of nonfiction material, there are such shows as *Biography* on the Arts and Entertainment channel. Other outlets that may offer you some possibilities are The History Channel, Discovery, and The Learning Channel. The material they present is much like magazine-feature writing.

There is another kind of writing that can be very lucrative and delivers a large audience. Some call it fiction and in many, many cases, the material is wonderfully bright, witty, cutting-edge, high-budget, and well-crafted. It tells a story in the briefest of seconds. The advertising spots that we all watch the Superbowl to see represent the top of the mountain for television advertising copywriters. But the term copywriter seems inadequate for the people who can tell us a whole story in thirty or sixty seconds.

Some of the stories, of course, aren't fresh or interesting. We've seen dozens of versions of the same material, such as tales of harried women looking for just the right cleaning, safety, sanitary, or cosmetic product.

But others are clever, fresh, bright, and memorable. Many times these high-budget productions that appear in the high-priced time slots don't tell us a story. They evoke a mood, share an emotion, provide a fantasy, or stimulate a daydream. To accomplish these things, a high degree of skill is required. And, for all you know, like someone who prefers poetry to novel writing, you may be better at writing thirty-second spots than full-length features.

Writing television commercials will require a background in advertising copywriting, and usually includes experience in ad agency work. It is also a highly competitive field and well-paid when you get out of the back room and into an office with a window.

You have little or no opportunity to weave in any personal ideas or philosophies. And, besides your boss and fellow staff members critiquing your work, there's the almighty client. They have the final say in anything you write, regardless of whether the Clio committee has already praised early drafts of your campaign. And an unsuccessful advertising campaign can lead you on a one-way trip to Palookaville.

Nonetheless, writing television advertising material has similarities to feature and television writing. Many of the same skills are required. As an advertising writer, however, you are much more severely restricted with regard to the usual narrative elements and to any personal statements you may want to make through your characters. But, since you're not restricted to a linear narrative, your fantasies can take many forms.

The flip side, of course, is that as a copywriter you are a flack for business and industry. You aren't trying simply to communicate to your audience, you're trying to convince them to try a specific product. The ethics of that is something you have to work out. The work itself is very creative.

And the fact that one of the top Hollywood talent/literary agencies connected with Coca-Cola says something about the blending of the various kinds of scriptwriting.

If you really want to write scripts, why restrict yourself to feature films? There are areas like advertising, industrials, and educational productions that can be fulfilling, creative, and well-paid. So, while you're nursing that screenplay each night between twelve and two, you might consider one of the other areas by day.

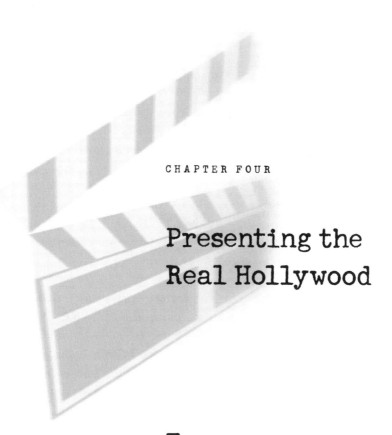

CHAPTER FOUR

Presenting the Real Hollywood

The biggest bank in town was looking for an assistant manager. Michael had all the right experience and knew he was the man for the job. When he heard of the opportunity through a friend, he asked his friend for a personal introduction. Then Michael learned everything he could about the bank. He asked his friends in the business; he researched the company. On the morning of the interview he was ready with his own questions and rehearsed them as he shined his shoes and picked a minute piece of lint off of his lapel. By the end of the day he had the job.

You probably don't want to work at a bank, even if you're working at one this very minute. You want to write. And why not? You went to school. You read Hemingway, Isak Dinesen, Fitzgerald, maybe John Updike, Donald Barthelme, and Sylvia Plath. The short biography that accompanied whatever you read by them in your textbook probably said something about how they sent off their manuscripts and *instanto presto,* they were discovered as geniuses and began a life of fame, fortune, and maybe notoriety. Well, except that Hemingway and Plath both did themselves in and Fitzgerald's books stopped being published before he stopped writing—

otherwise, respect, admiration, groupies, and getting by the doormen at the hip clubs was their lot in life.

Those biographies leave a lot out. Take it from a former publicist who's written tons of such promotional material. You leave a lot out for a variety of reasons, one of which is that no one wants to read about the long hard struggle. Unless, like Alex Haley, getting down to your last ninety cents just before the magic call comes from a publisher (whether true or not) is the defining twist the press agents put on the book promotion biography.

Think about the story that opened this chapter. Becoming a writer is more like getting the job at the bank than anything you may have read about in your old lit textbook.

Okay, you're not that naïve. You've watched *Biography,* you've tuned in to The History Channel, you know those writers didn't pop onto the world stage overnight. But they did write something and send it off to a publisher or a magazine editor and get "discovered."

In reality, writing, like getting a cushy job at a bank, is about being prepared when the opportunity comes along. It's knowing the field as thoroughly as possible. And, given the speed with which business changes, consolidates, merges, shifts, and folds up, bankers looking for work are forced to be as creative as writers, albeit they must direct that creativity onto different problems.

We all realize that getting jobs in the "real world" takes the appropriate education, training, preparation, knowledge of the field, and a willingness to keep up with changes. Why do so many hopeful writers think none of this applies to writing success?

It's Not a Tumor, It's a Business

Before we discuss some of the specific strategies that will help you succeed, there are a couple of things we need to repeat about the motion picture business.

Filmmaking is a business, a commercial enterprise in which companies worry about expenses, overhead, capital investment, planning for the future, and disastrous products. They watch the bottom line very closely— unfortunately sometimes after the fact.

Studios make movies for many reasons; almost all of them are money. Prestige, winning Academy Awards, and creating or contributing to a company's solid reputation are also reasons studios make movies, but generally they come second. It isn't studios that struggle for years and years to get an unusual, quirky, profound, or unique movie made, as Wendy Finerman did with *Forrest Gump.*

Why then are some really awful movies made? And why does a top box-office darling bamboozle a studio into backing a pet project, even if no one likes it but the actor's mother? Because studios think they can make a profit on it.

Additionally, people who work in the movies, like careerists everywhere, are concerned with getting ahead, making the right decisions, looking good to the bosses, gaining notice, obtaining promotions, and getting bigger paychecks. And in the case of Hollywood, many people in the business are star struck. Not only do they want all the rest, they want the opportunity to rub elbows with famous actors and be a part of the more glamorous aspects of the industry. The people who make decisions about the output of writers, directors, artists, actors, and all the others who comprise filmmaking crews don't see themselves as part-time teachers helping people become better writers or actors. They expect professional work to cross their desk. They don't have time to see a spark of something in one of your scripts and use their weekends and evenings trying to shape your writing into next year's Academy Award winner.

Helping Yourself

What, then, can you do to increase the odds that you will succeed in this highly competitive and exciting field?

Getting some education will probably help tremendously, although you never want to assume that because you've taken a couple of scriptwriting classes or attended one of the top film schools that you somehow deserve some kind of break or will be automatically successful. But taking classes at schools that have film departments can help you get a handle on this field, and, by taking scriptwriting courses, you can master the basics of this craft. This is especially true if the faculty has actual experience in the industry. Getting a degree in film studies is also an option, but not a necessity. The two major schools in the Los Angeles area do feed many of their graduates into the field.

How can you gain knowledge about the actual movie business? The best way to achieve an understanding of this field is by picking up and moving to Los Angeles. Once there, get a job, any job, in the industry. Or, if that's not an option for you, volunteer your services at the best company you can find that will take you up on the offer. Find out what films are about to start shooting and call around to see if you can work as a production assistant for free. Some film companies take on unpaid interns. Lots of student productions look for volunteer help; call one of the film schools in the area.

Observing first-hand and up-close is a strategy that's hard to beat. More specifically, a job on the creative-development side of the business that yields information about how scripts are discovered, culled from the piles of submissions, and developed into projects that can be produced is an ideal situation. Working in the legal department can provide solid information about contracts, and accounting can give you a peek at what kinds of deals are cut for the various freelance workers in the business. But working on the creative side or in production is probably the most profitable for your goals as a writer. Here you can see how stories are put together.

While you're giving away your time or slaving away at a real job, you might sign up for a writing class or two, either at one of the colleges or with the many private classes that are offered around town.

Getting Dialed In

Just living in Los Angeles where movies are a major presence is preferable to trying to succeed from a village in the Midwest or New England.

Barring your ability to actually take up residence in the city of angels, in order to storm the fort, it will be an advantage if you can get noticed by people in the business. So, if you have any connections whatsoever in the industry, ask them for help. If you develop a good rapport, keep in touch with them. Even if you don't develop a good rapport, if you feel their advice can be helpful, keep in touch with them. Maybe your aunt works for some producer at one of the studios or the independents. Call her. Maybe your father went to college with a guy who's now working at one of the production companies. Call him. Even if he works for a law firm that handles some entertainment companies, he's bound to know a thing or two about the industry. Maybe you haven't seen an old friend of yours in years and heard at your last high school reunion that she works in the business. Call her. Most people love being asked for their advice, whether or not they eventually take a genuine interest or help you with your career. Oftentimes people whom you contact can give you names of other people to talk to and then you're on your way. Talking to various people will give you some feeling of how the business operates. And remember, it is a business.

Better yet, once you've made a good contact, try and get to Los Angeles and visit that person. Usually when it's suggested that they go to Los Angeles, writers sigh deeply and confess to hating Los Angeles, or hating the traffic. They express concern about the crime or the bigness of the place. What's really happening is usually fear—fear of looking like an idiot, fear of high-speed freeway traffic, fear of getting lost, and fear of the irritation and stress that result from trying to find addresses in an unfamiliar and hugely spread out city. There's the fear of rejection, of feeling like the small tadpole in a very large pond. And there's a hate of Los Angeles just because it's Los Angeles. Everyone feels more comfortable in their hometown where they know their way around and feel that they have some contacts. But if you really want to succeed at this, you've got to go. At the least, you've got to visit, get a feel for the place, and meet whatever contacts you've managed to establish. Those contacts might very well lead to other contacts and other people to talk to.

Another long distance way to gain some knowledge and background in the industry is to keep abreast of the field by subscribing to one of the two industry trade papers, *Variety* and the *Hollywood Reporter*. And now, with the Internet, there are many sites devoted to Hollywood information. (More about these topics later.) You'll want to tune into these resources. What you want to get from your reading and research is an understanding of the industry. Generally, think of yourself as applying for a job at the bank. You know that you must prepare yourself for a job at the bank. Does work in Hollywood deserve less? You know it doesn't—this *is* your life, right? Enough said.

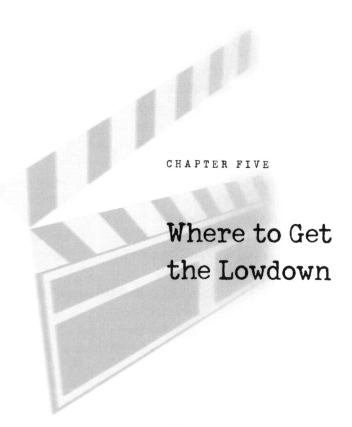

Where to Get the Lowdown

Hollywood is full of contradictions. It's both tacky and refined, home of the worst and best movies, and it is both cruel and nurturing for artists of various specialties. It is the primary place where you experience rejection from agents, producers, and studios. It is also the place where you can find nourishment and comfort. Others share your interest and understand your plight because they have similar ones. It is the best place to gain knowledge about your craft and become a part of it.

After beating on doors, trying to get one to open, there are things you can do that may help you along your way. And what with the Internet and the increasing availability of film classes around the country, in the future you may not even have to be in Hollywood to stay attuned, attached, alert, and aware of the flow of the business.

It's a Script Thing

One way to increase your writing confidence is to know what professional scripts—scripts that have been produced—look like, how they read, and what kinds of stories they tell.

If you live in the Los Angeles area and want to browse through scripts without actually laying down any hard cash for them, the Academy of Motion Picture Arts and Sciences and the American Film Institute (AFI) both provide libraries that include film and television scripts. Their libraries are open to the public. AFI's reading room is open from 10 A.M. to 5 P.M. Monday through Thursday; The Academy's scripts are available from 10 A.M. to 6 P.M. weekdays except Wednesday.

If you're willing to spring for copies of your own, the better to study and mark up, there are several stores in the Los Angeles area that sell them in their real form; that is, on regular bond with brads binding them. The following are the three most prominent companies that offer scripts for sale:

Book City sells their scripts for $15 unless they exceed 150 pages, then the charge is $20. You can call and order one with a Visa, Mastercard, or American Express card and they'll mail it to you. The mailing cost is $5 for each screenplay with $2.50 added for each additional script ordered. Television scripts are only sold at the Hollywood store.

- Book City, 6627–31 Hollywood Blvd., Hollywood, CA 90028; Tel. (323) 466-2525 and 308 N. San Fernando Blvd., Burbank, CA 91502; Tel. (818) 848-4417

Script City is a mail-order company that offers scripts, film books, screenwriting software, audiocassette seminars, and other merchandise. You can get their catalog for $3; it includes all the products they offer.

- Script City, P.O. Box 1500, 8033 Sunset Blvd., Los Angeles, CA 90046; Tel. (323) 871-0707

Hollywood Collectables is another mail-order house that will sell you a script in its raw form. They charge $15 for television scripts and $20 for features. Buy four scripts and the fifth one is free, buy eight or ten and you get two or three free, respectively. That price includes shipping and handling. You can call them for a catalog.

- Hollywood Collectables, 120 S. San Fernando Blvd., #446, Burbank, CA 91502; Tel. (818) 845-5450

No, It's a Book Thing

For the past sixty years Larry Edmunds Cinema and Theatre Bookshop, an independent, has specialized in volumes about entertainment. The store has just about any book you need in the field and if it doesn't, the staff can get it for you. They also can order a script if that's what you need. There are some exceptions, and you've got a better chance of getting the screenplay if it's contemporary, but they can fill most orders. You can find them at:

- Larry Edmunds Cinema and Theatre Bookshop, 6644 Hollywood Blvd., Hollywood, CA 90028; Tel. (323) 463-3273

Speaking of bookstores, if you can't find what you need in your neighborhood store, there are a couple of other places in addition to Larry Edmunds that specialize in industry books.

These two bookstores are true specialists:

- Samuel French Theatre and Film Bookstore, 7623 W. Sunset Blvd., Los Angeles, CA 90046; Tel. (323) 876-0570 and 11963 Ventura Blvd., Studio City, CA; Tel. (818) 762-0535

There are other places that carry many, many books related to writing, directing, and the movie business in general, but they also have other kinds of material. Stores that carry books you might find helpful include the following:

- The Writers' Computer Store, 11317 Santa Monica Blvd., Los Angeles, CA 90025; Tel. (310) 479-7774. (More about this store later, in chapter 9.)
- Book Soup, 8818 Sunset Blvd., Los Angeles, CA 90069; Tel. (310) 659-3110
- Op-amp Technical Books, 1033 N. Sycamore Ave., Los Angeles, CA 90038; Tel. (323) 464-4322

There is another hybrid store that's worth mentioning. Enterprise of Hollywood sells some books, but, more importantly, also has all the stationery materials that writers need, like script covers, paper, brads, and all the rest.

- Enterprise of Hollywood, 7401 Sunset Blvd., Hollywood, CA 90046; Tel. (323) 876-3530

Of course, Amazon.com, Borders Books, and Barnes and Noble are on the Net. You probably already know how to contact them, but just in case you've forgotten, you can find them at *www.amazon.com, www.borders. com,* and *www.barnesandnoble.com.*

Or It Might Be a Magazine and Trade Paper Thing

If you don't care about picking the scripts you read, but want a steady supply without buying them individually, there's *Scenario.* Since 1995 this quarterly magazine has published four screenplays in each issue. The screenplays vary from just-released films to classics, or at least past hit films, and they also include an unproduced screenplay. The work offered is supposed to be the writer's draft of the piece. Subscriptions are $49.95 a year. They can be reached at:

- *Scenario,* 3200 Tower Oaks Blvd., Rockville, MD 20852; Tel. (800) 222-2654

There are other magazines and newsletters that offer some comfort, information, and aid for your pursuit of writing work. Keep in mind that you shouldn't read too many success stories in these magazines. Just read enough to spur you toward your goal (and maybe your own interview one day), but at the first sign of feeling overwhelmed when you sense your confidence is draining away, stop.

Most of these magazines offer writing tips, industry news, often an interview with a writer who has recently sold material, sometimes an article by a script consultant or analyst or similar insider, and other miscellaneous information.

Probably the most solidly professional-looking, stable, and established of the screenwriters' magazines is *Written By,* a product of the Writers Guild. This magazine, formerly *The Journal of the Writers Guild of America,* regularly features a couple of interviews with writers, either newly emerged or well established; discusses Guild topics; features short articles on writers' issues, problems, and experiences; and covers miscellaneous topics of interest to screenwriters. The tab for a year's subscription is $40. If you believe in the idea that one way you can get closer to your goal is to visualize yourself being a successful writer, having lots of information about the Guild will encourage more realistic imaginary scenarios. To reach them, contact:

- *Written By,* Writers Guild of America (WGA), 7000 W. Third Street, Los Angeles, CA 90048; Tel. (323) 782-4522; e-mail: *writtenby@wga.org*

Creative Screenwriting, a six-year-old magazine that is published six times a year, bills itself as the magazine for the professional, not the wannabe screenwriter. It features articles on writing and focuses on the development of scripts to make them salable. On the back pages it runs a listing of all the spec script sales and pitches for the previous month or two. You can get a subscription for $29.95 or you can pick up a copy at Borders Books, Barnes and Noble, Waldenbooks, or various independent bookstores. For information, contact:

- *Creative Screenwriting,* 6404 Hollywood Blvd., #415, Los Angeles, CA 90028; Tel. (800) SCRN-WRT or (323) 957-1405

The bimonthly *Scr(i)pt,* which until 1995 was *Screenwrite Now,* has changed more than its name; the membership side of the organization has been discontinued. In this magazine you'll find articles similar to other screenwriting magazines, but beginning with the January 1998 issue, the magazine includes a listing of various script contests around the country. It's now an annual offering in the January issue. It goes for $29.95 for a year's subscription. Otherwise you can usually find copies at Borders Books, Barnes and Noble, and other upscale outlets. Contact *Scr(i)pt* at:

- *Scr(i)pt,* 5638 Sweet Air Road, Baldwin, MD 21013; Tel. (410) 592-3466

The quarterly *Fade In:* magazine is in its fourth year of life. The magazine was an outgrowth of the Writers Network group but it is now on its own, although the two organizations cosponsor events. *Fade In:* originally focused on writing, but has broadened its coverage and now also covers the ins and outs of the business, how it works, and what's going on. The cost of a year's subscription is $19.95; two years is $26. *Fade In* plans to go bimonthly.

- *Fade In:* 289 S. Robertson Blvd., #465, Beverly Hills, CA 90211; Tel. (800) 646-3896 or (310) 275-0287

For the past eighteen years screenwriters have had yet another source of information and shared wisdom. *Hollywood Scriptwriter* features interviews on the craft and business of the industry as well as interviews with writers. A subscription to the monthly trade publication goes for $35 in the United States and Canada, $50 for all other countries. To contact them:

- *Hollywood Scriptwriter,* P.O. Box 10277, Burbank, CA 91510; Tel. (818) 845-5525; Web site: *www.hollywoodscriptwriter.com*

SPAWNews (No, it has nothing to do with the movie or comic strip) is the monthly newsletter of the Small Publishers, Artists, and Writers Network. It features news of upcoming organization events, members' achievements, and articles that provide helpful hints and writing tips. A subscription to the newsletter is $15.

- *SPAWNews,* Small Publishers, Artists, and Writers Network, P.O. Box 2653, Ventura, CA 93002-2603; Tel. (805) 643-2403

The Scriptwriters Network has published a monthly newsletter for the past eleven years. It covers what's going on in the industry, membership news, and a couple of regular columns, including a summary of the group's monthly meeting and speaker. To get the $40-per-year subscription, contact:

- *Scriptwriters Network Newsletter,* 11684 Ventura Blvd., #508, Studio City, CA 91604; Tel. (213) 848-9477

There are a couple of other magazines of a more general nature. Both *Film Quarterly,* published by the University of California at Berkeley, and *Film Journal International,* published by Sunshine Group Worldwide in New York, will satisfy your need for other kinds of film information.

Film Quarterly publishes discussions and critiques of recent films. So, if you would like to take a break from structure, characterization, and plotting, you can pick up this journal and see what their writers have to say about the symbolism, the artistic merit, or the political, psychological, or philosophical implications of certain films.

- *Film Quarterly,* Press Journals, University of California, 2120 Berkeley Way, #5812, Berkeley, CA 94720-5812; Tel. (510) 642-9917

Film Journal International features articles on the industry, exhibition, producers, distributors, international news, reviews, and trends. The February issue includes the "Blue Sheet," which lists all planned upcoming film production. A one-year subscription goes for $50.

- *Film Journal International,* Sunshine Group Worldwide, 244 W. 49th Street, New York, NY 10004

More important than general magazines with regard to finding useful material that may directly aid your quest are the two trade journals, *Daily Variety* and the *Hollywood Reporter.* Both cover the business five days a week. It is in these news outlets that you can find out who just sold a big script; if a new agency is forming; which agents have, in *Variety*'s terms, "ankled" their present agency for a new one; which studio chiefs have left and who has taken over for them; and much more about the daily world of the industry.

They also write of new companies that have formed and usually include information regarding the type and number of films the new companies hope to produce. Both publications also run box-office and television ratings reports, gossip columns, and want ads (though don't expect to get a really good job through any of the ads).

- *Daily Variety,* 5700 Wilshire Blvd., Los Angeles, CA 90036; Tel. (800) 552-3632. Annual subscription: $219
- The *Hollywood Reporter,* 5055 Wilshire Blvd., Los Angeles, CA 90036; Tel. (323) 525-2150. Annual subscription: $219. Web site: *www. hollywoodreporter.com*

Maybe a Directory Will Help

Though they don't feature page-turning prose, directories can supply helpful information about the industry. If you want to know where to contact a writer or a director, for example, you can get the directories from the writers' or the directors' guilds. They can be reached at:

- Writers Guild of America, 7000 W. Third Street, Los Angeles, CA 90048; Tel. (323) 951-4000. Cost for nonmembers: $20 by mail, $17 if you pick it up at the office. If you send for it, include in the address: Attention Membership Directory Order.
- Directors Guild of America, 7920 Sunset Blvd., Los Angeles, CA 90046; Tel. (310) 289-2000. Cost to nonmembers is $23.82.

Hollywood Creative Directory, which began publishing in the early 1990s, offers a directory of all the production companies, from the major studios to one-man operations, doing business in Los Angeles. They list all the pertinent script personnel at a company; their phone numbers; and whether they do commercials, television productions, or features. Often included are the titles of some of the movies and/or television shows completed by the companies. The directory is published three times a year. Recently they have added directories of distributors, agents and managers, and others.

The *Blu-Book,* published annually in January by the *Hollywood Reporter,* is a standard directory that's been around for years. It isn't specifically aimed at writers, however, but at people who want to put a movie together and are looking for equipment and personnel such as gaffers, animal trainers, and camera rentals.

The Pacific Coast Studio Directory is the granddaddy of the directories. Small in format and price, the directory is published four times each year and goes for $10 apiece.

Hollywood Creative Directory, Blu-Book, and *The Pacific Coast Studio Directory* are generally carried by Larry Edmunds and Samuel French, or for direct ordering, you can find them at:

- *Hollywood Creative Directory,* 3000 Olympic Blvd., #2525, Santa Monica, CA 90404; Tel. (310) 315-4815 or (800) 815-0503; e-mail: *hcd@hcdonline.com;* Web site: *www.hcdonline.com.* Cost: $49.50 for a single issue; $120 for a one-year subscription
- *Blu-Book,* The *Hollywood Reporter,* 5055 Wilshire Blvd., Los Angeles, CA 90036; Tel. (323) 525-2150. Cost: $59.95
- *Pacific Coast Studio Directory,* P.O. Box V, Pine Mountain, CA 93222-0022; Tel. (805) 242-2722; Web site: *www.studio-directory.com*

One of the more interesting directories, focused exclusively on writers, is the *Hollywood Literary Sales Directory* published by In Good Company Products. Released annually in January, the directory lists what scripts sold in the past year, a one-line synopsis of the plot, how much they sold for, who sold them, and to whom they were sold. The directory also lists all the pitches and books that were bought. The information is arranged in various ways so that you can easily find information by agent, title, or buyer. In this directory, the reader can discover what stories are being bought and who in Hollywood is buying them.

An update is published in mid July. This $59.95 directory will open your eyes to the possibilities of making a nice piece of change for your script. The update runs $15.95. You can pick up the directory at various stores around the country, but it may be easier to order it directly.

- *Hollywood Literary Sales Directory,* In Good Company, 2118 Wilshire Blvd., #934, Santa Monica, CA 90403-5884; Tel. (800) 207-5022; Web site: *www.hollywoodlitsales.com*

Getting It Together

Writing is an isolated and isolating occupation, and after years of spending so much time with only a word processor for company, many writers' social skills are rustier than a junker in Jersey. That's only one reason why writers' groups can be a good thing for a screenwriter. There are other reasons as well. Some groups allow you to present your work, and they give you critiques. Most hold annual writing competitions, seminars with people in the industry, host monthly speakers, and workshops that can give you new ideas and at which you can pick up some information you may be able to use. And there is always that magic word of the last fifteen years: networking. Most every writers' group provides for networking. You meet people who know people who know people. And the people you meet, in and of themselves, can be worth meeting. Sharing writers' problems can diminish their significance. Getting to know others who do what you do, despite the natural competition among you, is more often than not a positive experience. And, besides, by encouraging others in their careers you'll wind up with a lot of contacts when they all, you included, move to the next step.

Writers' groups can be found listed on bulletin boards at the better bookstores. Sometimes there are listings in the book section of the Sunday newspaper (or whenever your local newspaper runs their book reviews and news). Attending lectures by visiting writers or Hollywood teachers can also provide opportunities to discover people who belong to writing groups. Bookstores feature appearances by writers with newly released books. Mixing with this crowd might turn up people involved in writers' organizations. The local library is also a place to look for possible groups to join. Writers attend college writing classes and may also belong to writers' groups.

It's difficult to recommend specific writers' groups because they form and dissolve, tend to be relatively unpublicized, and, in some cases, you have to be invited into the group.

The following groups are large and don't require an L.A. address to take advantage of all the member offerings. The Small Publishers, Artists, and Writers Network, mentioned earlier under its newsletter, *SPAWNews,* is an organization that includes novelists, nonfiction writers, scriptwriters, and artists. Each of its four chapters holds monthly meetings that often feature speakers from the industry. They meet to improve their writing and for fellowship. Membership runs $45 yearly and includes a subscription to the newsletter.

Writers Network, the group that originally produced *Fade In:* magazine is a busy bunch that doesn't meet often just to gab. For $125 per year (that includes a subscription to the magazine) they offer a script library, script analysis and notes, and a help line that you can call with script or script-selling problems. They also hold an annual screenplay competition, and a midsummer pitch festival at which you get the opportunity to pitch your project to over a hundred agents and producers. As a member you also get discount tickets to the annual fall and summer seminars that feature top industry people. The group publishes an agency guide that covers only literary agents and includes notes indicating what kinds of material the agents are looking for.

- Writer's Network, 289 S. Robertson Boulevard, #465, Beverly Hills, CA 90211; Tel. (800) 646-3896; Tel. (310) 275-0287

The Scriptwriters Network is a five-hundred-member, nonprofit, all-volunteer organization for writers. They hold a general meeting the second Saturday of each month to which industry speakers are invited. They also offer a producers' outreach program for connecting up writers and producers. They do staged readings, hold scriptwriting competitions, and offer various other advantages for struggling writers, most of whom are not produced. Membership is $60 per year and includes a subscription to the newsletter.

- Scriptwriters Network, 11684 Ventura Blvd., #508, Studio City, CA 91604; Tel. (213) 848-9477

For the Keyboard Challenged

If your skills with a word processor or typewriter are less than sterling you can always take your material to a professional typist. Despite the widespread use of personal computers, typing services still exist. If you have your material in some sort of format and can convey to a pro what you need, she can probably get it in presentable shape for you. It's no surprise that in the Los Angeles area there are many companies to help the keyboard-challenged writer. Glancing through any of the writers' magazines and newsletters, especially the Writers Guild journal, *Written By,* you will find at least a dozen advertisements for typing services.

Back to the Basics

If you don't feel your skills are yet ready to go it on their own, if you fall into that category of people who are always looking to improve on what they've got, or if you're just looking for a warm room where you can share your writing woes with others in a similar situation, you can check out writing classes.

Most colleges, universities, and community colleges offer at least one screenwriting class, usually more since the great American screenplay has replaced the great American novel as the goal of many writers.

If you really want to sink your teeth into studying film and get into first-rate writing classes, there are the standard schools that most everyone in the business considers the holy three. As Yale and Harvard are to law, these schools are to film studies. You can contact them for program specifics. Two of them offer graduate degrees with a specialty in writing.

The University of California at Los Angeles (UCLA), a large state university in west Los Angeles, offers undergraduate degrees in film and television and an M.F.A. in screenwriting. Competition is very tough. The graduate writing program is small and highly respected. It funnels lots of writers into successful careers and provides lots of personal interaction with faculty and other writers. Professors Richard Walter and Lew Hunter have both written screenwriting texts.

- University of California at Los Angeles (UCLA), 405 Hilgard Avenue, Los Angeles, CA 90024. Film studies: Tel. (310) 825-5761

The University of Southern California, a private institution in downtown Los Angeles, offers a B.A. degree in film and television production, a B.F.A. in film writing, and an M.F.A. in screenwriting.

- University of Southern California, School of Cinema-Television, 3450 Watt Way, University Park, CA 90089; Tel. (213) 743-2736

On the opposite side of the country lies the third school: New York University. This private, four-year school is located in the heart of New York City and offers a B.F.A. degree in film, television, radio, and video. There is no specific screenwriting major. An M.F.A. degree in film is offered.

- New York University, Tisch School of the Arts, 721 Broadway, New York, NY 10003. Undergraduate film: Tel. (212) 998-1700; graduate film: Tel. (212) 998-1780

Another school of excellent reputation is the American Film Institute. Their Center for Advanced Film and Television Studies offers a program in screenwriting. Completing the one-year program can earn you a certificate of attendance, but if you already have a B.A. degree, you can earn a master's at the completion of the two-year program. Students without undergraduate degrees do not receive college credit for courses taken here. As with the other leading schools, the competition is stiff. To find out more:

- American Film Institute, Center for Advanced Film and Television Studies, 2021 N. Western Ave., Los Angeles, CA 90027; Tel. (323) 856-7628; Web site: *www.afionline.org*

The advantage of attending the preceding schools isn't simply the instruction, the opportunity to study with other bright, talented students, and the opportunity to rub elbows with people actually working in the industry. There are also lots of special events, presentations, and extracurricular film-related activities that you can participate in and take advantage of.

Of the larger four-year schools whose undergraduate enrollment in film studies exceeds a hundred students, there are several that offer degrees, an emphasis, or special programs in screenwriting.

Chicago College, a relatively small private school, boasts a rather large film department with seventeen hundred students enrolled at last count. Students who choose screenwriting complete a core of lower division classes that includes a couple of writing courses. The last two years focus on advanced screenwriting and writing related classes.

- Chicago College, 600 S. Michigan Ave., Chicago, IL 60605-1996; Tel. (312) 663-1600

Columbia University has one of the oldest and most distinguished film programs, with a faculty that includes such writers as Larry Gross (*48 Hours*) and Janet Roach (*Prizzi's Honor*). The graduate writing focus is a three- to five-year program that includes various writing classes, revision classes, and workshops. The completion of two feature scripts is required, one of which serves as a thesis project.

- Columbia University, 2960 Broadway, New York, NY 10027-6902; Tel. (212) 854-2815

Drexel, a private, four-year school, which emphasizes internship programs that provide real-life experience, offers a B.A. in dramatic writing. Drexel blends a broad base of liberal arts classes with professional courses. Each student must have a six-month period of full-time employment to write a feature film or television show.

- Drexel University, 3141 Chestnut Street, Philadelphia, PA 19104; Tel. (800) 237-3935

At Loyola, screenwriting is one of five areas of emphasis students can choose. The undergraduate program requires fifteen lower-division writing classes and upper-division classes that include writing, editing, adaptation, and directing. The school also encourages its students to take classes outside the writing area.

- Loyola Marymount University, 7900 Loyola Blvd., Los Angeles, CA 90045; Tel. (310) 338-3033

At Northwestern, Dr. Chatman has directed the creative writing program for the past eight years. Although the creative writing program doesn't limit itself to screenwriting, it is part of the film department, and most students opt to work in this medium. The undergraduate course is open to juniors and seniors after they complete the lower division core.

- Northwestern University, 1905 Sheridan Rd., Evanston, IL 60208; Tel. (847) 491-7315

At Rochester Institute of Technology, Howard Lester, chairman of the film department, oversees the scriptwriting program. The course includes four levels of screenwriting classes that require the completion of an independent production and a feature-length thesis project.

- Rochester Institute of Technology, 1 Lomb Memorial Drive, Rochester, NY 14623; Tel. (716) 475-2779

The School of Visual Arts offers a four-year program in which students can choose to concentrate on screenwriting beginning in their second year. Studies include screenwriting clinics, the business of screenwriting, and other writing-related classes. A feature-length work written with a mentor is the final requirement.

- School of Visual Arts, 209 E. 23rd Street, New York, NY 10010; Tel. (212) 679-7350

Beyond these institutions, there are dozens of schools around the country that offer degrees in film; film and video production; film, radio, and television; or some combination of several of these. Most of these schools don't emphasize screenwriting. Their curriculua are divided equally between studies in film production and in film history, theory, and aesthetics.

Other Classrooms

If you already have a degree, if you aren't looking for a complete program, or if you're looking for individual classes in writing, you should check out the universities or colleges, including community colleges, close to you.

If college classes don't appeal to you or require more commitment and cash than you can muster, there are always the short-term writing classes that are held around Los Angeles and around the country by people recognized by the industry. These teachers offer short-term workshops, held on weekends or over four or five weeks. Some emphasize a particular approach. If you can't take their classes, you can find their books, and in some cases, audio tapes.

- Syd Field, 270 N. Canon Drive, #1355, Beverly Hills, CA 90210; Tel. (310) 271-1839; e-mail: *Fieldink@Screenwriterscorner.com*
- Michael Hauge, Hilltop Productions, P.O. Box 55728, Sherman Oaks, CA 91413; Tel. (800) 477-1947 or (818) 995-4209; e-mail: *Hilltopproductions@juno.com*
- Robert McKee, Two Arts, Inc., 12021 Wilshire Blvd., #868, Los Angeles, CA 90025; Tel. (310) 312-1002; Web site: *http://www.mckeestory. com*; e-mail: *contact@McKeeStory.com*
- John Truby, Truby Writer's Studio, 751 Hartzell Street, Los Angeles, CA 90272; Tel. (800) 33-truby or (310) 573-9630; e-mail: *johntruby @aol.com*; Web site: *www.truby.com*

Writers Boot Camp, created by Jeff Osborn, guarantees that if you sign up for the six-week camp you will go from story idea to first draft of your screenplay. Classes meet once a week, and in your contract you have to promise to spend at least ten hours outside of class working on your project. After the classes are finished, you have two weeks to finish up. Then you get coverage and a conference with the instructor. Writers Boot Camp has campuses in New York, Chicago, San Francisco, and Los Angeles.

- Writers Boot Camp, 2525 Michigan Ave., Bldg. I, Santa Monica, CA 90404; Tel. (800) 800-1733 or (310) 998-1199

More Help

One of the must-read books among Hollywood writers and studios is *Making a Good Script Great* by Linda Seger. Linda, the author of four other books, holds seminars around the country and around the world. She is also a script consultant for producers, production companies, and writers. It can be worth your time to seek her advice about your screenplay. She can be reached at:

- Linda Seger, 2038 Luella Ave., Venice, CA 90291; Tel. (310) 390-1951; Web site: *http://members.aol.com/lsmgsg/mgsg.html*

The editor of *Hollywood Scriptwriter,* Lou Grantt, is also a consultant who has worked with production companies and individuals. You can reach her at the magazine's address or at:

- Lou Grantt, *http://ourworld.compuserve.com/homepages/lgrantt,* or you can let Yahoo! do it by going to *www.yahoo.com* and searching on "Lou Grantt."

In addition to the preceding, there are also lots of programs offered year 'round in Los Angeles. It's one of the advantages of living in the Big Orange, and why people in the industry will always advise you to move to Los Angeles if you want to write. In fact, there's an old saying that you have to live in Los Angeles until you make it, then you can move out of town.

One seminar offered by the Motion Picture Academy is the Visiting Artists Program. Well-established writers such as Lowell Ganz, Babaloo Mandel, and Bo Goldman spend an evening speaking about their experiences as writers. At the end of their talks they take questions from the audience.

This past year for the first time, U.S.C.'s School of Cinema and the Writers Guild co-sponsored "Writers on Genre," a summer discussion series that featured such writers as Ron Shelton, Brian Helgeland, and Bob Farrelly. The point is, beyond writing groups that regularly hold meetings with industry people, the schools also offer classes and workshops. Even bookstores and libraries occasionally present seminars for writers. You just have to keep your eyes open, your ears pricked, and, oh yes, live in L.A.

CHAPTER SIX

Getting to "Fade In"

Ona day while I was accompanying a friend to look at a house for sale, the salesman, assuming we were together, asked us what we did for a living. She gave him her job title. Then he looked at me. I told him I did a little teaching. He dismissed me immediately, probably figuring that a teacher would never be able to afford the house we were touring.

After we left my friend asked why I hadn't told him I was a writer, specifically, why didn't I tell him I was a screenwriter.

I explained that anyone who dares admit they're a writer gets a mix of answers, but in our movie- and TV-dominated culture, scriptwriters are guaranteed to hear at least a couple of responses (neither of which I wanted to deal with) if they admit what they do.

Professional Secrets

The first is, "you (or 'they') ought to write a television series about this job." It doesn't matter what jobs people have: working in a flower shop, a fast-food restaurant, or an insurance office, most think (except maybe accountants) that really funny things happen at their jobs and that their occupational trials and tribulations are interesting enough for a TV series. Or, maybe these people are looking for a little understanding from the world—especially if they work in a service job—about the battles they face every day to get their work done. Maybe they just want to be the center of the universe—a desire that seems to be growing like, or with, the Internet.

The other response you're almost guaranteed to get if you reveal your profession is a variation of, "I have some ideas you should write," as if writers hang around like panhandlers waiting, nay, pleading, for people to donate writing ideas. Every writer who isn't permanently or temporarily written-out has a dozen ideas he would love to get to if only he didn't have to complete the current project or if he didn't have to spend so much time on a day job.

One variation of the second response that writers often get is the comment, I've got a lot of ideas. I wish I could write, or I've got a couple of ideas I want to write when I can find the time. The truth is these people will never write.

There're at least a couple of careers that share an occupational handicap. Since we've all attended a little or a lot of school, too many people think they know about teaching—how easy it is, how it should be done, and how it isn't what it used to be. Much the same applies to writing. Sometimes it's fun to imagine what it would be like if everyone were mathematically oriented and our common communication transpired via numbers rather than words. Then writing and using the English language would have the hint of mystery that numbers now enjoy.

Let's face it, if you're a mathematician or a physicist, no one you meet on the street assumes that if they only had the time they too could develop a unified field theory or explain the particle-wave conundrum. But everyone, or nearly everyone, is certain that they've got the best screenplay ever within the confines of their imagination just waiting for that moment when they have the time to jot it down on paper.

Writers themselves often contribute to the problem. By adhering to the professionals' tacit creed that whatever their endeavor, they must make it look effortless, they further the notion that writing isn't a craft that needs honing. And while the man on the flying trapeze makes his profession look effortless, few people want to climb up and give it a try. Not so with writing.

Some writers even go on television and tell how their latest projects poured out with alarming speed, complete and full-blown. They don't mention the tedious rewrites, the trouble with the computer, the fact that the whole first act needed a complete rewrite after having been analyzed by a professional script reader, or that they gained ten pounds from sitting all day for months on end.

While no one but a few fellow writers wants to hear the painful details of what other writers experience while trying to put a 120-page, big-screen blockbuster on the page, the truth of writing is quite different from the fantasies of nonwriters. And that includes many in Hollywood who will tell you they're working on a script. Press them to show you the pages, and they will confide finally that their stories are mostly "up here" and point to their heads.

A writer is one who writes as well as talking about what she wants to write. Do you want your tombstone to say that you had lots of ideas but never got around to putting them on paper? Or do you want your obituary to list all the scripts you've actually written? Don't forget that old cliché about the road to hell.

Taking action after you get a story idea is the first decision point that divides the nonwriters from the writers. Nonwriters never do anything about their ideas; they just let them roll around in their heads, convincing themselves that their ideas will eventually be fabulous films. But you've already passed that demarcation point. You're ready to write. You've scheduled it into your life. So what to do now?

Testing, Testing

You need to test out your story idea(s). See if it works, see if you can hang 120 pages on it, see if it has any dramatic potential, see if it has any freshness, uniqueness, interest. Don't underestimate this task. It's not easy, but by the time you're finished, you'll have half the job done.

The very first thing you should do with your idea is write it down. All you need to do is write a four- or five-sentence paragraph explaining the story. This requires that you think through those four or five lines. It's here that you realize writing really is a magical event. Some ideas sound terrific in your overworked imagination but reveal their threadbare selves when you try and put them on paper. Thinking and writing are so inextricably connected that this exercise will reveal to you whether or not your idea has what it takes to become a screenplay. While it rolls around your brainpan, interrupted by other thoughts, dreams, or trying to remember where you left the car keys, it may sparkle and glow. But putting it on the page strips it bare and exposes its lack of logic, believability, and intrigue.

If writing it down doesn't make the idea disappear from embarrassment, and you still think you've got something, your next task is to ask yourself, "Where can it go?"

One would-be writer was always coming up with new ideas and thought each was hilarious or perfect for a mystery story. But he never asked himself the important question: And then what? Can you come up with the *and then what?* for your idea? Here's an example. There's a narrow alley between two skyscrapers that dips down to both buildings' first basement levels, then comes back up to ground level at the other end. A street-level walkway connects the buildings. What if every time a cop drove through there, something happened to him and he came out the other side changed in some way? Okay. So what? *And then what?* What story are you going to tell here? This barely qualifies as a genuine idea.

One acquaintance was fascinated by this idea: Every time people put their bags on the conveyer belt that goes through the airport security screening machines, something happens, something is stolen out of them, or something is placed in them. But where can you go with that?

Both of these ideas might become a part of a script, but neither are ideas that can carry a screenplay. Unless—repeat: *unless*—you do a lot of building around both of them. In short, you have to create an entire story around them.

Here's another question to ask of your idea. *What's the story going to be about?* Some ideas just don't seem to shimmer with story potential. A former student wanted to write a script about a woman who had been physically abused by her mother when she was a child. So, what's the story? Are we going to be treated to a dozen scenes of child abuse? That's not a story. There are dozens of stories that might be told with this idea. Which one are you going to tell?

Take It for a Drive

Take your idea out and drive it around a little. See what other people think of it. Watch their reactions as you tell them. Let other people add their two cents worth. You don't have to use any of their suggestions, but what they say might give you some ideas about how to develop your grand vision.

Just one proviso: Don't talk about your new idea too extensively. You don't want to risk talking it to death.

Run this test by your idea. Compare it to what's playing at the theaters in your town. Do you have an idea for a movie about comets or asteroids hitting the earth? Ummmm . . . Where have we seen that before? How about one where the real truth never seems to be clear, but there are definitely people or aliens or people from beyond the grave trying to scare you, tell you the truth, or do you in? Another ummmm. Have you been watching too many episodes of *X-Files*?

When Hollywood script analysts read such material they label it derivative because it seems derived not from real experiences, i.e., from life, but from other TV shows or movies. It's not fresh, it's not new, and the reader has read stuff just like it a hundred times.

Once you've finished the tests and have deemed your idea unique and clever enough to pursue, warm up the computer again. Now you are going to expand your idea to three to five pages detailing the story.

This exercise has a couple of purposes. It lets you see if your idea has the seeds to grow into a full-length screenplay. If you can't see where this idea might go, you can drop it, change it slightly, or rework it from the premise up.

If the original idea or its revision has potential, then writing the four pages will clarify where the story's going and how it should be told. When you finish this exercise, read the pages several times. Get the feel of the story. Read the pages to friends and relatives. Get their responses. Don't be afraid to do this. It's very helpful. Your listeners will tell you when they're confused. They'll ask why a character is doing what he or she is doing. They'll bring up lots of things you may not have thought of when you wrote it because you were so thoroughly inside it you missed something obvious. Listen, don't talk.

The best thing about doing this brief treatment is that you've actually taken a step toward writing the screenplay. The three to five pages aren't necessarily easy because at this stage you're doing a lot of creating—you're actually writing the story of the screenplay. You're thinking it through.

Work on these pages until you're satisfied with them, then do a master scene outline. Use the treatment as a guide, and jot down, on index cards or not, the scenes you'll need to get to the final climax and dénouement. This exercise is another involving task that requires real creative work.

The outline will let you see the story movement through each act. Don't toss off the outline quickly. This is another step in thinking through the story carefully, and, although you're spending more time gazing into space than hitting the keyboard, this is writing.

If you prefer not to write an outline, then write an expanded treatment. You can even do both. You do the same thing in the treatment that you do in abbreviated form in the outline. You're working out what scenes are needed, where they should be, how the subplot(s) will work in, and how the all-important climaxes will work.

Once you get this work done, again, let other people read it. Your friends' feedback will give you clues as to where you've gotten off-track or haven't made yourself clear. Take their comments and revise where you think it's needed. Refine it further. Now that you've got the story down, you can enrich it. You can layer and texturize it.

At this point you've done about half the work of getting it on paper. The difference, the crucial difference, between nonwriters who talk about writing and those who keep a daily date with their word processor is that doing it requires that you think things through. There's nothing like committing something to paper to see how inconsequential, trite, uninvolving, or preachy it is; or how brilliant, profound, and funny it is.

Writing a short treatment forces you to take a lump of narrative clay and begin shaping it. It forces you to confront the material and see it for what it really is. So, as soon as you start putting your story on paper, you'll see the work you need to do. Then you're on your way.

Look It Up

Once you make these basic decisions about your story you'll need to do some research, if it wasn't research that led you to your idea in the first place. Note: if you're writing about an historic event, place, or person, you'll need to do your research up front. Otherwise you won't have enough information about the subject to make an outline.

But, if you're writing something contemporary, once you get the outline, you can see what you need to research. We can assume that people interact with each other in very common and familiar ways no matter the setting—if they didn't then we couldn't have television sitcoms. But each profession or job has different responsibilities, requirements, conditions, and trials. If your story revolves around two garbage men, you better do some research to see how they work, what drives them crazy at work, what their goals are each morning when they begin their rounds, and what conditions prevail in their world. If you're featuring a television newsman in your screenplay, get to know a little about how that profession works. You've got to see it from the inside. If an important historical event takes place during your story or a nationally important event has influenced your characters, you'll want to refresh your knowledge of that event.

The same holds true for specific props and other elements in your script. If you have materials that are important in your script, you better know the properties of those materials. For example, do you have a character in your script who's going to escape from a building on nylon thread? Would it hold him? Would it cut his hands to pieces? Could it possibly work at all? You as the writer need to know that. If your story involves young children or groups of people you don't encounter every day, then, again, you need to do research into how their lives are lived.

One writer had a script that included the crash of a small private jet. She interviewed an employee of the Federal Transportation and Safety Board to learn step-by-step how that agency conducts its investigations. She also wanted to get a look at the Safety Board's office. She needed to know something about basic aerodynamics and generally how planes behave in crashes. It helped her create a truer picture for those scenes in her story. It's this sort of research that strengthens a screenplay.

There's another form of research that will improve your script. Perhaps you have no interest in history. Your story, set in a world you know backwards and forwards, is very contemporary. Regardless, you'll want to make sure that any references you make, even to contemporary things, are accurate. Maybe you've never watched *Seinfeld,* but one of your characters has. You figure you've heard all the popular lines from the series and can throw one in. If you're not absolutely sure whether it's a line associated with George, Kramer, or Elaine, you'll want to check to make sure you have it attributed properly. It's not a big thing, but you always, always, always want to be 150 percent as perfect as possible.

Researching also applies to characters. If you feature a character that has a distinct style of speech, an accent, or speaks with a combination of English and a language native to that character, find a real-life example of your character's speech. Listen and take notes. The more accuracy, the truer the feel of the piece. Good research endows your story with a truer feel, and it will garner better reactions from all who read it.

Testing out your ideas and researching will save you a lot of effort unless, of course, you prefer to keep your ideas as mental toys that you pull out when your work or life gets unbearable. Daydreaming can be very reassuring, comforting, and mentally refreshing. Man is blessed with the ability to spin fantasies. But we can't confuse them with writing.

Now you're ready to type "FADE IN" and step closer to your dream.

CHAPTER SEVEN

Screen and Teleplay Formats

At every writers' workshop I've spoken to, in every class I've taught, there are always questions about format. Students worry that they will make some minor mistake and it will cost them. Format is so detail-specific that they're sure they've missed something important. They rarely have, but it is a good idea to review the basics.

Why is there so specific a manner of putting a screenplay on the page? Beyond tradition, there are the needs of a future film crew to consider. The word "CONTINUED" lets the actor, the assistant director, the director of photography (D.P.), and the editor know the scene continues to the next page. Creating a common language and approach is the basis for developing a consistent format. Think for a minute of the last book you read. You already knew how to read it. The layout is exactly the same for every book you encounter in the English language. You also recognize poems when you see them in print because of the way publishers have established their presentation.

When scripting films came along, there was no editor between the writer and those whose job it was to translate handwritten, messy, or unintelligible but brilliant copy into a readable form. Every script had to act as the finished product. That left editing, spelling, grammar, and form up to each writer. What chaos would have ensued if no agreements had been reached. Readers, from script analysts to the loftiest of producers, needed to have some assurance that there would be a continuity of presentation from one script to the next.

What if each time you picked up a book the first thing you had to do was figure out how it worked? Would it be back to front? Front to back? Top to bottom? Would the lines of type run right to left? You would be forced to read the book's organization before you read the book. So as narrative script-writing developed over the years, certain matters of format developed.

Some things are still included in scripts that probably aren't necessary, like capitalizing sound effects. Modifying a script is so easy today, what with computers, that there hardly seems the need to continue the capitalization of sounds to be heard on screen. In the studio years, these were capitalized so that the sound editor and the sound effects team could skim through a script and quickly know what kinds of noises they would be responsible for supplying. Now, however, with the number of revisions a script goes through from writer to finished screen product, it's hardly necessary to alert the soundman in the first draft of the project. If the writer gets a chance to rewrite the work, it's still usually several versions away from shooting script form. But capitalizing the sound effects in the first draft continues.

The essential element to remember about format is this: Your script must look like the most professional scripts going across agents' and producers' desks if you want to get it read. If it looks like an amateur product, or if you're sure your story is so brilliant that readers will overlook your incorrect format, think again. There's one caveat here. Not all professional, salable, produced screenplay writers follow format *exactly* the same way. But they conform pretty closely to the standard.

Given the number of scripts crossing the desks of production companies and agents, any reason not to read one is usually good enough for a story editor or reader to disqualify it. And if yours isn't formatted it might get the boot.

So, let's talk about format. Unlike those books devoted to format, those instructors who live and breath format correctness, who assume that one minor error is tantamount to script death, let's be rational and realistic about the whole thing. I usually only spend one class period on format for my students, and most of them get it the first time out. Don't over-agonize about the mechanical aspects of scriptwriting. Concentrate on writing a great story.

The following is based primarily on my years as a script analyst, during which time I reviewed over five thousand scripts arriving in the offices of more than nine different production companies and film studios.

Covering It

Let's start with feature-film scripts. And further, let's start at the beginning, literally: the cover for your masterpiece. This is an opus that will run somewhere between 100 and 130 pages—unless it's a TV miniseries (which you will have noticed they aren't doing many of anymore). You have three-hole-punch paper and you'll hold these pages together with two, yes, two brads—one in the top hole and one in the bottom. No spiral binders or those semipermanent binders allowed!

There are a couple of approaches you can take with the wrappings. Although there are some upscale covers that look like fake leather and have the title imprinted in them, these aren't necessary. They may be overkill. The reader will secretly wonder if you're trying to dress up a mediocre effort.

One of the most common script covers is heavy stock paper (about sixty-five to seventy pound) with a pre-fold imprinted so that the brads you use to bind the pages are inside, and hence protected by the cover. Most agencies and studios use this type of cover. Readers like them because the brads are covered, which prevents them from scratching desktops or catching on everything, including the other scripts that are in the big stack that has to be read overnight.

If you don't want to send off to a store in Hollywood for your covers, using heavy stock paper is fine. Avoid bright or neon colors. White is common, so are various shades of gray or beige. There's even some green and navy blue. Just punch it with three holes and bind it together with the pages. You don't need to put anything on the cover. If an agent agrees to represent you, the agency will rebind your script in their covers with their logo on it. Once a studio owns your script they will usually send the script to their reproduction department and it will be reformatted to that company's specifications, and they'll supply covers with their logo on them.

You can even be more minimalist than this. You can simply use the title page of your script as the cover. No one will gasp with shock that your script doesn't have a cover. It will be treated the same as other scripts. The downside of this approach is that scripts tend to fall apart. The cover sheet gets pulled this way and that, and, before you know it, it has ripped away from the brads. Then, the same thing begins happening to the first page of your story. Once the title page is gone, so is your identification and contact numbers.

Just remember, covers shouldn't call too much attention to themselves, and they should be neat and clean. Don't use college term paper covers or those covers that are used for business reports.

Remember the Titles

After a reader opens the cover of a script they should see the title page. Put the title of your screenplay around a third of the way down from the top of the sheet, centered. Don't worry whether you've come down from the top of the sheet twelve or twenty-two lines; it's just not that big a deal. Below it, triple spaced and centered, type, "by" or "an original screenplay by." Triple space and print your name.

Because computers offer so many fonts, script titles aren't necessarily printed in all caps Courier anymore. But, I wouldn't let this opportunity to use other fonts get out of hand if I were you. Keep it simple and readable, keep the size under control, and don't forget that you're presenting yourself as a writer, not a graphic artist. Sticking with Courier, boldface, maybe in fourteen to sixteen point rather than twelve is probably the best advice. But it won't matter if the title's in Times Roman, so long as the script's printed in Courier.

Down in the lower left corner you will type your name, address, and contact numbers—each on a separate line. I have also seen scripts in which the contact names were in the right corner, but generally they're in the left. If you get an agent and she sends it out, she'll put her contact information on the left. If you have a production company, print its name following your name in the stack of information. Sometimes the contact information is preceded by the word "contact" followed by a colon.

If you're adapting a book, that should be noted. Double spaced under your name you should write: "adapted from (or based on) the book (title) by (author's name)." If you've adapted a story, just replace the word "book" with "story."

If you and a friend or a friend has created a story, but you've written the script of that story, note that in the script, depending on the kind of contract you and your friend have made with each other, with the following notation, triple spaced below the title: "Story by Joe Smith and Bill Jones" or "Story by Joe Smith." Double spaced below that, add "Screenplay by Bill Jones."

Many script manuals tell you to put the title in quotation marks. I personally think it's a redundancy. We know this is the title of the script, we're not referring to the title in the middle of a long essay on our work, so what do you need quotation marks or underlines for? Does the title of this book have quotations around it on the cover? No. I never saw a script rejected or disregarded because it either had or didn't have quotation marks around the title.

Remember, don't date your script, don't note that it's been registered with the Writers Guild or the Copyright Office, and don't indicate which draft of the script this represents. With regard to drafts, no matter how many times you write a script, the one you show to agents and producers is considered the first draft. If they buy it, it will undoubtedly go through subsequent drafts, which will be noted on the title page. Remember that the title page should be pristine—no typos, no spelling errors. Each time you present the script, you should run off a fresh copy; at least make a new copy of the title page.

The following pages show samples of the preceding information.

The Insides

The page following the title sheet should be page one of your script. Don't include a cast of characters, a famous or obscure quotation, a dedication, a synopsis, a proposed budget, artwork, or explanatory notes to the production company that's reading it.

Set your machine to put page numbers in the upper right hand corner of the page. Don't forget. You'll want to know the exact length at some point, you won't want to get the pages confused or out of order, and most of all, the first thing readers do when they pick up a script they've been assigned is look at the length.

You don't need to do a title header on each page as newspapers and magazines put slug lines on the articles writers submit. Unlike copy that will be emended by an editor and so needs to be unattached to other sheets, the script is bound; it won't be edited like newspaper copy.

The word "CONTINUED" or "CON'T" at the bottom and top of each page

GUN SELL

by

William J. Smith

Contact:
William J. Smith
0000 W. 187th Ave.
Los Angeles, CA 90000
Phone: (310) 888-8888
Fax: (310) 888-8887
E-mail: WJS@SOS.com

GUN SELL

an original screenplay by

Bill Jones

William J. Jones
0000 W. 187th Ave.
Los Angeles, CA 90000
Phone: (310) 888-8888
Fax: (310) 888-8887
E-mail: WJJ@SOS.com

GUN SELL

by

William J. Smith

Adapted from the novel *Gunsel*

by Ramona Chandler

William J. Smith
Talking Pictures Prod.
0000 W. 187th Ave.
Los Angeles, CA 90000
Phone: (310) 888-8888
Fax: (310) 888-8887
E-mail: WJS@SOS.com

GUN SELL

An original story by

Bill Jones and Joe Smith

Screenplay by

Bill Jones

Contact:
William J. Jones
0000 W. 87th Ave.
Los Angeles, CA 90000
Phone:(310) 888-8888
Fax: (310) 888-8887
E-mail: WJJ@SOS.com

is also unnecessary. We know to turn the page when we get to the bottom. Some manuals explain that "CONTINUED" is used when a scene continues to the next page. When this is done, it is written inside parentheses and typed at the right margin at the bottom of the page and again, without parens at the left margin at the top of the page on which the scene continues. You can use it or not. I've seen more scripts omit it than include it. However, there are times when you definitely want to use the abbreviation "CON'T"; we'll get into that a bit later.

Avoid numbering the scenes. Whether or not to include this is a question I'm asked over and over. At this stage, you don't need to number each scene, and you most assuredly don't need to include that same number on the opposite margin. This numbering of shots is done when the script's broken down by the unit production manager or assistant director and a shooting schedule is created. In this early version of your story, the inclusion of these shot numbers is distracting.

When you're setting up your pages there's something else you'll want to remember. Script pages need to have a good balance of white space and text. If a script is too description-laden, it's off-putting. If it has too much dialogue readers know it's going to be too talky without enough action and visuals telling your story.

Your challenge is to keep your descriptive paragraphs short and to the point. You'll also want to intersperse your dialogue with description or camera and scene directions.

Following are three pages. Two are examples of unbalanced script pages; the third is the way an ideal script should look.

Sample #1

INT. UPSCALE RESTAURANT - EARLY EVENING

Harry and Mary, an attractive, elegant couple about 35-45 years old. They follow a HOSTESS to a well appointed table by the window. The couple sits.

                         HARRY
              So what about it?

                        MARY
I don't know, what about it?

                        HARRY
You mean you won't give it back?

                        MARY
For hell's sake, I didn't take it.

                        HARRY
Yes you did.

                        MARY
No I didn't.

                        HARRY
Did.

                        MARY
Didn't.

                        HARRY
I'm telling Mom.

                        MARY
Go ahead. She knows I didn't
do anything wrong.

                        HARRY
Ya did too. Yesterday I came
home from Little League. You
were mad and grabbed my glove.

                        MARY
Nanny nanny pooh, pooh. Did not.

Sample #2

INT. A DARKENED ROOM - NIGHT

Lit only with the glow of a streetlight. Lots of expensive, antique furniture and accessories clutter the room. A MOAN breaks the silence. Then

>   WOMAN'S VOICE
>   Man, oh God no.

There's silence. Then another MOAN. A door to a lighted hallway opens. Three FIGURES dressed in tight fitting clothes and ski caps come into the room. They step carefully around the furniture.

One of the figures goes to a window and quietly opens it. Four FIGURES, dressed the same as the first, crawl into the room through the window. Each figure goes to a spot in the room. When they all reach their assigned place, one of them raises his arm straight over his head and after making sure the others are watching, he swings it down like a pendulum.

At that all the figures begin searching the room. Drawers are opened and searched through. The wall is felt down. Pillows on chairs and a couch are turned over and inspected. One figure climbs up to the chandelier and checks it. A rug is rolled up. A grandfather clock is opened and checked.

One figure moves into a darkened corner. Odd unidentifiable sounds come from the darkness. One sounds like a gun being cocked. Then there's a raspy sound.

On the other side of the room one figure stifles a SNEEZE. Two others climb up to the ceiling in opposite corners. It's not clear what they're doing.

Without warning there's the sound of a shoe scraping on a wooden floor. All the figures stop dead still and hold their breath. They all wait. No further sound is heard. Slowly they take up where they left off.

Sample #3

EXT. A CLIFF PATH - MID MORNING

VICTORIA, carrying a white cane, walks the cliff path approaching the bench. DESMOND rushes out of the house and down the steps toward her.

                    DESMOND
                 (calling)
             Victoria! Victoria!

Victoria stops and turns toward him.

                    DESMOND (CON'T)
             Olivia says you fired her.

In the background Olivia comes out on the balcony in a skimpy outfit and watches the scene with satisfaction.

                    VICTORIA
             Desmond please. I've been
             trying to talk to you for days
             about this. But you won't even
             give me a minute of time.

Desmond reaches Victoria.

                    DESMOND
             I explained that.

                    VICTORIA
             I don't believe you.

                    DESMOND
             So you fire Olivia because I
             didn't talk to you?

He turns and shares a exasperated look with Olivia.

                        VICTORIA
              I didn't fire her, Molly's
              returning. I don't need her.

The first sample is dialogue heavy. Its saving grace is that the speeches are short. The second is weighted down with too much description. Don't despair. Not every single page of a script can be perfectly balanced, nor should it be. But keep it in mind so after you've finished your screenplay, while you're doing one of your rewrites, you'll remember to pare back those long descriptions and endless dialogue scenes.

Now that we're clear on the wrapping and the general look of your script, let's briefly discuss more specific issues of format.

Details

When setting up your computer to input your screenplay, the left margin is one and one-half inches so it can be bound on that side and you can still read the copy on the page. The right margin is one inch. The margins for the top and bottom of the page are one inch. This applies to all but the first page. On that sheet you center the title at about an inch down from the top. A little more if you want, not much, a couple of lines maybe. Some writers include their names under the title, but in most of the scripts I've read, it was not included. I wouldn't.

Because the left and right margins are unequal, the entire layout is shifted to the right. The tabulations reflect this and are measured from the left margin. Tabs are used extensively in script writing. They are as follows:

- Scene introductions (called scene headings or scene slug lines), camera suggestions, and scene descriptions are all placed flush with the left margin.
- Dialogue is positioned fifteen spaces from the left margin.
- The parenthetical information that is sometimes placed under a character's name is twenty-five spaces from the left margin, or ten spaces from the dialogue tab.
- Characters' names are placed thirty spaces from the left margin, or fifteen spaces from the dialogue tab.
- About sixty-five spaces from the left margin is the spot for any "CUT TO:" you may need to include and for the final "FADE OUT."

An example of the proper spacing and tabulations for a page of script follows.

EXT. AN URBAN ALLEY - NIGHT

A BUM wanders into the alley, bumping into garbage cans and dropping his fifth of whiskey. He curses (AD LIB) when it breaks on the pavement. As he licks up the spilled booze, cutting his tongue and pulling out shards of glass, he hears a whisper coming from a dumpster.

                                 VOICE [*30 sp. from margin*]
                         (sarcastically) [*25 sp. from margin*]
               Want a chance to go to college? [*15 sp. from margin*]

The Bum looks at the dumpster uncomprehendingly. Then continues lapping up the whiskey.

                              VOICE (CON'T)
                     Ya don't wanna miss this great
                     opportunity.

                                  BUM
                     I don' talk ta dumpsters.

                              VOICE
                     Your loss, pal because in here
                     I've got a wallet with $20,000
                     in the secret compartment.

ANGLE ON THE BUM
                                  BUM
                     And I'd believe you 'cuz . . .

                              VOICE
                     Because it might be true.

The Bum comes over to the bin. He cautiously opens the lid and looks in. He opens it wider and leans in farther then he loses his balance and falls in head first.

Quickly the lid slams shut. The sounds of CHEWING are heard followed
by a LIP SMACK and a loud BURP.

                              VOICE
            Score!

The preceding indicates the tabs you need to set. There shouldn't be any
others.

The purpose of all the various techniques and terms used in scriptwriting
is to guide the reader through the work. In prose, writers simply describe
locations and tell readers what the characters are doing. Playwrights give
us a general description of what the stage will look like, then provide directions for each role.

The scriptwriter has to create each stage for the reader/viewer and tell
us what the characters and the camera are doing.

As a writer you have to locate the reader. The reader and later the viewer
must know where they are in terms of setting, environment, characters,
and atmosphere. Even if the screen is completely black, the audience needs
to know pretty quickly whether they're in a cave, a mine, a darkened room,
a windowless cell, or what. And they need to know in short order what is
going on in this dark place. A black screen without any action is not a film,
it's intermission. A writer can fool an audience, leading them to believe
they're in one place when in fact they're in another. But the audience needs
to feel they have an idea of what's going on; they need reassurance that
something *is* going on.

Once in a theater in Los Angeles the audience was fifteen minutes into a
confusing, not particularly interesting film. Suddenly the silence was broken when someone stood up and shouted, "Does anyone have any idea
what's going on?" We all clapped as the man walked up the aisle and out of
the auditorium. Subsequently most of us left the theater before this movie
was over.

To prevent that from happening, you need to learn the basic terms and
techniques that will enable the reader to follow easily the story you're
telling.

Editing

Every script begins with "FADE IN" and ends with "FADE OUT." "FADE IN" is the equivalent of "Once upon a time. . . ." Generally "FADE OUT" isn't used anywhere else in the script except the end. Sometimes, you can indicate a fade to black which is immediately followed by a fade to white screen or fade up. It's probably better if you just stick to using them only at the beginning and the end. After you make your first script sale and the movie makes money, do what you like.

There are different kinds of instructions to facilitate the editing of films besides "FADE IN" and "FADE OUT." Whether or not to include any of them is up to you, but most of them aren't necessary. Let the editor do his job.

The most common editing notation is "CUT TO:". If you put this at the end of every scene, it gets pretty irritating. I'd save it for when and if your film takes a very significant turn with regard to mood, tone, or scene type, like at the end of each act. Many scripts omit them completely; others use them at the end of master scenes. Flash cuts, flash pans, jump cuts, and such are also probably better left out or used very, very, very sparingly. You may want to occasionally use the dissolve. When you have, say, a close-up of a girl's colorful skirt blending into couples swing-dancing, you might want to indicate that this is a dissolve or overlap. Another one you might occasionally use is the freeze frame. Unless you're writing an old-fashioned comedy or a satire of one, you won't want to use an iris or a wipe. They're just not seen much anymore and when they are, they call too much attention to themselves and remind the audience they're watching a movie. When you use editing instructions, capitalize them and type them beginning at space sixty-five. All editing instructions are at the right margin.

Locating Us

At the beginning of the story and each time you change locations, you need to let the reader know. That is done by using a scene heading (or scene slug) which is typed in all caps. For example:

```
INT. HIP COFFEE HOUSE - LATE NIGHT
```

You always begin with "INT." for interior or "EXT." for exterior. Follow that with two spaces, then indicate the location. After this add a space, a dash, and another space, then list the time of day. This brief setting shouldn't run longer than one line. You can include more detail in the brief paragraph of stage instructions that follows the scene heading. For example:

```
INT. HIP COFFEE HOUSE - LATE NIGHT
A jazz combo plays a smoky TUNE but the crowd doesn't pay much
attention. GRETTA, 30ish, who looks like she consumes only sports
drinks, enters from the outside door and starts looking around. In a
dark corner a MAN rises from his chair and spills his coffee.
```

You nearly always follow a scene heading with some description of what's happening in the scene. Keep it short and concise. Single space it and begin it flush with the left margin. The first scene in a new location usually includes some description of the place. For example, if you have a scene in Chelsea Clinton's dorm room, you may want to give a brief view of what it's like. When you return to that setting later in the story there's no need to describe it again, unless there are differences that are important to the story's plot or characters.

In theater, lighting and the spoken word direct the viewer's attention. In film, the camera directs it. If it's important that once in Chelsea's room we notice that on the wall is a picture of Kenneth Starr with darts sticking in it, then you'll want to include a camera angle that will direct our attention to the picture. To do that you note the angle, using all caps and typing it flush with the left margin, thus:

```
ANGLE ON KENNETH STARR'S PICTURE or
CLOSE-UP OF A PICTURE OF KENNETH STARR
```

or it can be written:

```
CLOSE-UP
On a picture of Kenneth Starr. Darts stick in his face.
```

For descriptions of specific kinds of shots, refer to chapter 8. Remember to use them sparingly. The director of photography has to have something to do.

If you have long dialogue scenes, rethink them. If you're positive that a particular conversation is absolutely essential, break up the scene by letting the audience know with as few words as possible what the characters are doing while they're talking. Make sure they *are* doing something. Please, keep them away from tables and restaurants as much as you can. Movement of some kind is preferable. It's even better if what the characters do can be worked into the plot. Remember *Lethal Weapon 2*? In an early scene Danny Glover's character is adding a room on his house using an electric hammer when Mel Gibson's character comes to talk to him. Later on the hammer is used as a weapon in the heat of a battle. This is a very basic example. Rewatch *Charade* with Audrey Hepburn and Cary Grant for a better one.

Another way to break up the long dialogue is to occasionally put in a camera direction. There's a very good chance it won't be used if it isn't crucial to an understanding of the scene, but it will break up the page. It is, of course, always preferable to include camera angle directions if they *are* essential.

If you have characters moving from one setting to another without a jump in time, note on the new scene header that the time is continuous. As in:

```
EXT. SUBURBAN SIDEWALK - AFTERNOON
Two teenage girls race to the front door of a comfortable house
LAUGHING and GIGGLING. The taller one pulls out a key and lets them
in.
```

```
INT. COMFORTABLE HOUSE - CONTINUOUS
The girls close the door and run . . .
```

If you have one scene follow another in the same location but it's a few minutes or some time later, note this in the following manner:

```
INT. HARRY'S AMERICAN BAR - DAY
Silent as a graveyard. The bartender idly washes glasses while a
single CUSTOMER sits happily at the bar sipping a beer.
```

```
INT. HARRY'S AMERICAN BAR - LATER (or EVENING or NIGHT)
```

```
Raucous crowd fills the room with noise, movement, and gaiety. Some
wave the banners of a winning soccer team. The Customer seen earlier
```

```
sits slouched over the bar spilling his drink as he raises it to his
mouth.
```

You don't need to be specific about the time; day, morning, or night is usually fine unless an additional detail is important to the plot or mood. And if it *is* important to the plot, make sure you include it. Remember, you're leading your readers. They won't know what you don't tell them.

When your character is in a situation, usually a vehicle, in which there are interior and exterior shots within one scene, that's generally written:

```
INT./EXT. - BILL'S CORVETTE/HOUSE - EVENING
Bill quickly shoves a lipstick-smeared handkerchief under the seat
as he drives into the driveway. As he gets out of the car Nancy comes
out the front door.
```

If you're including a flashback, that is noted in the same way as a scene heading.

```
FLASHBACK - A 1960s DRIVE-IN RESTAURANT - NIGHT
```

When you finish the flashback, you write:

```
END FLASHBACK
```

and then you set up your next scene, or you write:

```
END FLASHBACK - RETURN TO SCENE
```

Scene headings will allow your reader to follow the locations of the story and the camera angles. Descriptions of action and place will enable them to know what is happening at each setting.

Dialogue It

When writing characters and their dialogue remember that characters' names are always capitalized and placed immediately above their dialogue.

```
                    TAYLOR
          You're going to do what with that?
```

Character names aren't centered over the dialogue. The name is set at thirty spaces in from the left margin. Dialogue, which is single spaced, takes up about the middle third of the space between the left and right margin. In other words, it begins fifteen spaces in from the left margin and ends about fifteen spaces before the right margin. Running each line of dialogue too close to the right margin looks messy, and it throws off the timing.

Any parenthetical material under the characters' names should be from-the-neck-up direction only. This includes the tone of voice the character uses or their facial expressions. The parenthetical material begins twenty-five spaces in from the left margin. Use these sparingly! If the actor can't figure out what kind of emotion you're looking for from the story that pre-ceded the dialogue, then maybe the story needs to be reworked, or maybe the actor needs to be replaced.

```
                    JEREMY
                 (pleadingly)
          No, that's not what I meant. You
          got it all wrong.
```

On the other hand, if a character walks to a table and gets a gun and fondles it, that material is dealt with like all other stage directions. It begins at the left margin, typed in upper and lower case and is single spaced. If the character reaches for the person he's pleading with and hugs her, that also is handled like regular stage direction. If a character's speech comes at the bottom of the page, the following is probably the best way to handle it. If you only have room for the character's name and one line of dialogue be-fore you start the next page, put the whole thing on the following page. If you have room for the character's name and two lines of dialogue, plus a line to put the abbreviation "CON'T" in parentheses, then begin the dia-logue on that page. At the top of the following page, put the character's name followed by the abbreviation again.

At the bottom of page:

>   BRANDON
>   I've been thinking, Angela. We can't
>   go on like this, it's time to say . . .
>   (CON'T)

and at the top of the next page:

>   BRANDON (CON'T)
>   . . . hello to a new life. I just won the
>   lottery!

Breaking up dialogue is awkward. The best thing to do is avoid it if possible. There is another instance in which you use the abbreviation of continued in parentheses. That is when a character's speech is interrupted by action description.

>   BRANDON
>   We'll take these over to Mom's.

He picks up a load of dirty clothes.

>   BRANDON (CON'T)
>   Tell her to burn them.

There are two important terms that apply to narration and dialogue: one is "voice-over" and the other is "off-screen." In the first instance, if you have a character who is not a part of the scene on screen, who is a narrator, that is a voice-over. If in your screenplay you have evil aliens plant cameras on earth, as they watch what the cameras transmit, we too watch, but what we hear are the aliens' reactions to the scene. You use the term, "voice over." It is written "(V.O.)" and follows the character's name. On the other hand, the second term is used if you have a character who is a part of the scene, but is not on screen. For example, a girl's date has come to pick her up and as he waits in the living room, she finishes dressing in the bedroom. While she's dressing they converse. This is an off-screen character speaking so it's written as "(O.S.)" and follows the character's name. Following are examples of both "(V.O.)" and "(O.S.)":

```
EXT. - A CITY STREET - DUSK

The street is crowded with drug dealers, muscled men preying on
senior citizens, and Wall Streeters.

                        ZARGOT (V.O.)
                From the monitor, it seems our little
                earth friends are more corrupt than we
                thought.

INT. A SMALL APARTMENT - EVENING

Clayton wanders around the pretty living room holding the cat and
glancing at the bookcase and the TV. From the bedroom

                        TIFFANY (O.S.)
                I'll be right out. I'm almost ready.
```

You want to make your script as easy to read and follow as possible, so you want to avoid breaking the story's continuity at the bottom of the page. If you don't have room to write at least one line of description following a scene heading, put the scene heading on the next page. In other words, a page shouldn't end with a scene heading without any descriptive text.

Once you set your computer for prescribed margins, you should have no problem. But don't change the bottom margin to accommodate additional material. If your script's running too long, do some paring. Every script can stand a little trimming.

Sing It

If you have a particular piece of music that you want as part of the scene, indicate that in the description. Remember, however, that for musical numbers which aren't in the public domain, production companies are required to pay royalties. If the material is that of a popular entertainer or is a contemporary classic, the price will probably be pretty steep.

If, on the other hand, you don't care what music is played, only that it be of a certain type to fit the mood of the scene, then indicate that in the scene description.

Music comes in two varieties, realistic, or referential, and background music. Referential music has an actual reference in the scene, e.g., a character turns on a radio and we hear the music from it, or a character goes into a club and a band is playing. You capitalize the name of the music if you're referencing a particular piece. Background music you already know.

Sound effects are capitalized. If you have a door SLAM and the audience will hear it, it's capitalized.

Title Cards

If you think it's necessary to locate the audience geographically with specific titles, indicate that in the script by writing the word "TITLE" in caps at the left margin, followed by a colon and the name.

```
TITLE: MOGIDISHU
```

If you have a sign actually in a scene, include it in the scene description:

```
The living room is decorated with balloons and streamers. On a huge
recliner sits a sign: FOR DAD.
```

Ending It All

Besides ending the script with "FADE OUT," flush with the right margin, some writers come down a couple of lines, center, cap, and underline "THE END." Other writers skip it. Some skip "FADE OUT" and just write "THE END." I've also seen scripts with neither.

The following might be helpful:

What to capitalize:
- FADE IN, FADE OUT, THE END
- CHARACTERS' NAMES OVER DIALOGUE
- CHARACTERS' NAMES THE FIRST TIME THEY ARE USED IN THE SCRIPT
- SCENE HEADINGS
- CAMERA DIRECTIONS
- SOUND EFFECTS
- EDITING DIRECTIONS
- CONTINUED

Margins/tabs (in spaces):
- 10 – Top and bottom margins
- 10 – Right margin
- 15 – Left margin
- 15 – Scene headings, scene descriptions, and directions
- 30 – Dialogue
- 40 – Parenthetical character directions
- 45 – Characters' names
- 65 – Editing notations

When to single space:
- Scene descriptions
- Dialogue
- Between characters' names and their dialogue
- Between characters' names and parenthetical directions
- Between parenthetical directions and dialogue
- Between dialogue and (CON'T)

When to double space:
- Between scene heading and scene description
- Between scene descriptions and characters' names
- Between the last line of dialogue and additional description, character direction, or camera angle
- Between FADE IN and the scene heading
- Between the last line in the script and FADE OUT
- Between paragraphs of lengthy scene descriptions

Television Scripts

If you are going to write a spec script for any hour-long television show, there are a couple of things to remember. You must know the characters well and how the show works. You should also know that many shows will not accept spec scripts for their shows. As a reading sample, you can submit scripts you've written for shows other than the one you're approaching. You can see why they might be wary. If this happens to you, the kind of script you submit should be for a similar show. If *ER* wants to see a sample of your writing, but not an *ER* script, send them a *Chicago Hope* script.

You can find out which shows are buying and the person at the company to contact if you subscribe to *Written By,* the Writers Guild magazine. In that publication, they list current television shows.

Hour-long television shows are written in four acts, each about fifteen pages long. Sometimes they include a teaser, of not more then three or four pages, at the beginning and a one-page or two-page epilog at the end. It depends on the show. Remember *Quantum Leap?* It always had a teaser at the beginning. So does *Law and Order.*

The beginning and end of each act is noted on the script, and you use "FADE IN" and "FADE OUT" to bookend each act. The title page begins with the name of the series. Double spaced below it is the title of your episode, in caps and underlined. Follow these with your name and contact information. See the samples on the following pages.

Many television scripts don't have covers, just the title page. It works because the scripts, at about sixty pages, aren't particularly bulky.

The first page of the script again includes the series title, the title of your episode, and "act one" (written out) centered at the top of the page in caps and underlined. In television, the names of the acts are always written out in full.

You do not need to number the scenes, although if you look at a produced hour-long script, they will be numbered. The production company will add the numbering and all the producers' names, etc., when they buy your material.

Other than these few things, hour-long television scripts resemble feature-film scripts, although television productions are more dialogue heavy than feature films. Let's face it, two actors standing and talking is cheaper to shoot (depending on the stars' contracts) than shooting complicated action sequences around Los Angeles. It's probably wise to note the level of action (Remember *Rockford Files* and *Miami Vice?*), the number of locations, and the size of the supporting cast the show you're writing for features. Write your spec script accordingly. Think of the difference between *Ally McBeal* and *X-Files.*

Following are sample television script pages.

Sitcoms and what they used to call (although the term hasn't been heard much lately) dramedies represent the greater deviation from standard feature-film format.

Half-hour shows are written in two acts. The scene breaks within those acts occur each time the story or location shifts significantly. The scenes

ROOM OF HOPE

NO EXIT

Written

by

John Paul

Your Name
Address
Contact Numbers

<u>ROOM OF HOPE</u>

<u>NO EXIT</u>

<u>ACT ONE</u>

FADE IN

EXT. THE HOSPITAL - NIGHT
An ambulance, SIRENS wailing, pulls in to the emergency and trauma center and comes to a SCREECHING halt. Two EMTs jump out. . . .

INT. THE EMERGENCY ROOM - CONTINUOUS

Doctors come running. . . .

FADE OUT

<u>END OF ACT ONE</u>

are assigned letters, beginning with *A*. The acts and scenes are noted on the script.

On the first page of your script you should put the series name and the title of your episode, centered, about an inch down from the top. Capitalize the series name, and, if you want, put the episode in quotation marks.

At the beginning of each act and each new scene, you come down a little less than a fourth of the page to start. Here you type, all caps, underlined, spelled-out, the act (or teaser). Come down a couple or so spaces and, centered, underlined, and capped, write the letter of the scene. Down from that about six or eight lines begin the scene. On act one, or the teaser, you begin with "FADE IN." Each act and scene ends with "CUT TO:".

In sitcoms, titles, scene designation, act designation, and scene headers are underlined and, along with the scene description/directions, are written in all caps. The dialogue in half-hour scripts is double spaced and begins after you double space following the character's name.

Parenthetical instructions are used more often, and they come at the beginning of the character's dialogue rather than centered beneath the character's name. If you have to split a character's dialogue between pages use the term "(MORE)" rather than "(CONTINUED)."

And, finally, the scene letter is included with the page number, usually immediately below it in parentheses. On the following page is an idea of how a half-hour script should look.

As a final note on this chapter, if I were you, I'd worry about the details of format after you finish your first draft. You don't want to let it get in the way of the free flow of your story in the rough draft. And then again, with the increasing use of software packages, format may soon cease to be much of a problem.

<u>SHOW TITLE</u>

"NAME OF EPISODE"

<u>ACT ONE</u>

<u>A</u> (<u>Scene A</u>)*

FADE IN:
<u>EXT. ALLEY – LATE AFTERNOON</u>
CHICK AND HAROLD ARRANGE A TRAY OF DELICACIES
FROM THE DISCARDED FOOD THEY PULL OUT OF THE
GARBAGE CANS.

                    CHICK
     (ENGLISH ACCENT) I think we can

     look forward to a sumptuous feast

     tonight.
                              CUT TO:

*can be written either way

CHAPTER EIGHT

Getting the Look You Want

Scenes from your script keep running through your head. You can see all the detail, or at least in some of your scenes you see all the various elements. You have a particular point of view of the scene. For example: You have a scene of a running man. In your vision, you see him in a field, in long shot, then you switch to a close-up of the bramble he's going to trip over, then back to medium shot. This is the vision you want to see on the big screen.

The reality you have to face is that there is a 99 percent chance that if this script of yours is purchased, developed, and makes it to the local theaters, the vision on screen will resemble what runs through your head about as much as Michelle Pfeiffer resembles E.T.

The improbability gives rise to the oft heard line, ". . . but I really want to direct." And it's exactly why writers hope to direct the material they've written. But here's the next catch. Even when you direct your own material—if you can reach that pinnacle—chances are that the ultimate screen version will have little in common with what's playing in your head as you write the script.

Why? The reasons are legion and have everything to do with money—the ruling force inside the borders of Cinema City. Money rules just about every decision made regarding everything from above-the-line people, down through the crew that's hired, all the way to the temporary production assistants (P.A.'s) who distribute the daily call sheet or keep the director supplied with Mylanta.

But you can't help getting pictures in your head. Your imagination is so visually oriented that they won't stop coming. And, hey, that's why you're writing screenplays instead of treatises on gene theory. Well, don't try to stop the images. Let them come, let them lead you, otherwise it's not nearly so much fun to write.

It might very well be that by the time the script you're working on is sold and put into production you'll be so old you'll be going to an Alzheimers' twelve-step program to figure out ways to remember who you are and how to find your way home. Some script you wrote years and years earlier will be an irretrievable memory.

Or, less depressingly and more realistically, you'll be five or six scripts removed from this one, and you won't remember specific images. So when the director decides to set the scene—which you had placed in the Ritz in Paris filmed in long, medium, and close-up shots, each suffused with sensuous afternoon sunlight—in a Denny's outside El Paso, shot exclusively in two shots at midday, you won't remember your original vision.

If neither of these eventualities occur, and if it happens that you get the work you've expelled from your imagination on screen before you've forgotten what you wrote, be prepared for pain.

What you see on the big screen won't match what you saw in your head. The point of view won't duplicate what you envisioned, the actors won't read the lines as you imagined hearing them, and the timing and placement of the shots will all deviate significantly from what you envisioned.

Unless you have the opportunity to take part in each and every stage of the production, and budget is of no concern, be prepared for surprises. But, think for a minute. How often has someone described something to you but when you actually experienced the thing described, it was completely different from what you expected? Remember the last blind date you had? Did you ever look at a rental house you saw described in the want ads? Okay, you get the point. Consider the following:

```
FADE IN

INT. TYPICAL GOVERNMENT COURTS BUILDING - DAY


A cavernous, empty, marble-lined lobby, two stories high with a
circular stairwell at one end. GUNSHOTS rend the stillness and echo
through the building. Silence. Then more GUNSHOTS.


A nicely dressed, tiny, gray-haired WOMAN timidly opens one of the
office doors and looks around. The clatter of FOOTSTEPS running down
the stairs is heard. The Woman steps into the lobby just as a MAN'S
figure appears around the curve of the stair.


He raises his gun shooing her out of his path and comes down the last
few steps slowly. The two stare at each other.
```

Take the above passage and ask three friends to describe what they see and how they see it. You'll get three very different visions. One person might see something that looks like it could be the background for a Tennessee Williams' play with close-ups of the anguish on the characters' faces. Another might see something that could be like a John Grisham novel. Still others will see something very New York City or very Moscow, or will call up images of a courthouse with which they are familiar. The characters, how they look and dress, will also elicit a variety of responses.

The description isn't specific enough to lead the director, director of photography (D.P.), art director, costumer, and set decorator to fulfill what you've got in your head. So give them a break. And we didn't even mention the producer who will cry and whine at every dollar spent. He will try to use whatever location is the cheapest to rent and do the scene in one take.

The alternative is to write Dickensian description. That will guarantee you a screenplay of, say, three hundred to four hundred pages which will never be read.

A second alternative is to get yourself involved in the production. However, previous writers have ruined it for the rest of us. Most productions want to dispense with the writer a.s.a.p. It seems a cruel thing to do to ignore a resource that could be a great help. But it's done all the time. No one will pay the writer any mind even if he or she is on the set. Usually no one wants the writer around for various reasons.

There's ego, of course. In this case it's often the director's. He regards the script as raw material upon which he will imprint his own style, ideas, visions, and philosophies *ad infinitum nauseam*. You would think the director thought up all this material himself, just as later the audiences will think the actors are making up the words they repeat for the camera.

It isn't always bad that the director takes possession of the material and makes it his own. Often a director can take material and make it something more wonderful than it was originally.

Often the director, producer, and crew don't want the writer around because he will whine about the many ways the production is deviating from the original conception which he, by this time, has come to regard as second in importance only to those two stone slabs Moses found freshly fired on Sinai. (And, do you ever wonder just how much reinterpreting of that material Moses did?) So the writer, with his gnashing of teeth, constant tears, contrary attitude, and discontentment becomes a royal pain in the ass. Everyone eventually wants to get him on a flight to Fiji, pronto.

Short of becoming a real producer-writer, one who will be on the set and do meaningful work, as opposed to someone who's a producer in name only (producer being a Hollywood title that's apparently handed out to anyone who has the temerity to ask for it), you have to do your best to convey as much information as possible that can be understood by a director, cinematographer, art director, and others on the crew. Later on when you're directing your own material, or at least having some input as a producer-writer, you may not need the following information, but for now, the following terms will help you communicate with the people who will be molding your work for the big screen.

The Shooting

The following terms shouldn't be overused—give the D.P. a little credit, he may know better than you how to shoot a particular scene so that it will have the impact you want. That goes for the director too. Give him credit for understanding the emotional center of a scene and supplying a few ideas of how to reach it successfully, even if it isn't shot the way you wrote it. Let them do their work, don't overload them with instruction. Scripts have been written without any shot suggestions. However, sometimes you'll determine that a scene calls for specific shots—you figure it's the only way to communicate the information you want conveyed in the scene. A sensible approach is to save the very specific instructions for a few crucial scenes.

For example, if you have two characters in a coffeehouse talking, you'll probably want a two-shot. But, if one of them hears a voice off-screen and responds to what that voice is saying, then you'll want to add: "ANOTHER ANGLE" or "ANGLE ON . . ." if you want the audience to see to whom your character is talking.

After you've finished your script go back through and consider the look and sound of each scene. Then add in camera movement, placement, and various instructions to the script. Remember, don't overdo it. As for those instructions, the following should explain or remind you of what they are.

Camera Angles

Establishing Shot: This is generally a long shot coming at the beginning of a film or a scene that establishes the time and place of the action. *The Fugitive* opened with a long pan of Chicago at night. The shot located us as to the time, place, and tone of the film. Even if you start your film in a tight, close shot, at some point you have to let the audience know where they are. *Back to the Future* took an interesting approach to the establishing shot. In it, Marty got on his skateboard and rode through his small town. We learned everything we needed to know to locate ourselves in this story.

Long Shot: This is a relative term, but generally a long shot is taken from far enough away that it includes the landscape or a building or a large exterior. How many times in *Die Hard* was the full shot of the building taken? That's a long shot. The shots of the police, the FBI, and various other law enforcement people gathered at the foot of the building are also long shots.

Medium Shots: Basically there are three. A medium-close shot is from the mid-chest up. A mid-shot cuts the figures off just below the waist, and a medium shot is from below the knee up. You don't have to be this specific. Remember our two people in the coffeehouse? Shooting them in the booth and showing their full figures is a medium shot. Getting a little closer is also considered a medium shot.

Close-Up or Close Shot: A close shot ranges from shots taken of a subject from the chest up to having the character's face fill the screen. Generally a close-up is called for if you want the subject of the shot to fill the entire screen, i.e., a car, the dog, the gun, well, you get the idea.

The above four shots are basic. But there are others that get more specific and should be used sparingly and with care.

Extreme Long Shot: Remember the opening shot of *Aliens* or *Sound of Music*? Those are extreme long shots. So were several scenes just before the aliens attacked Earth in *Independence Day*. Sometimes these are called wide angle shots.

Extreme Close-Up: If a close-up shows the subject's head and top of his shoulders, then an extreme close-up shows just his face. If it's important for the audience to see something, like say the key in *Notorious* or the stolen money in *Psycho* or the electric hammer in *Lethal Weapon*, then you want to do a close-up. But if the condition of the object, or its characteristics is important, then include an extreme close-up. The mouth in *Rocky Horror Picture Show* is an extreme close-up.

Full Shot: In this shot the subject (human figure or an object) is entirely in frame. In *A Perfect Murder* Michael Douglas' character is shown in full shot, from head to toe, several times.

Two Shot: This shot includes two figures. It's probably not really necessary to specify this when you put the finishing touches on your script because it will be obvious from the scene you're writing that there are two and only two characters in the picture.

Three Shot and One Shot: Same as the previous description except, well, you've already figured it out.

Over-the-Shoulder Shot: This is usually a two or three shot in which the camera is placed behind the shoulder of one of the characters and favors (focuses on) the character opposite. The camera can also favor one of the two characters in the scene without being over-the-shoulder. Remember Billy Crystal in *The Search for Curley's Gold*, the one he produced? If the camera had favored him any more often than it did, it would have been a one-man show.

Point-of-View Shot: This is a useful shot to include in your screenplay. If your character witnesses a murder and we see the murder from that character's perspective, then you need to include the notation that this is a "POV shot." Again, in *A Perfect Murder* Michael Douglas' character watches, and we watch with him from his POV, as his wife comes out of her office and goes to get into her car.

Low-Angle Shot: In this shot the camera is set low and is angled up on the action. Oftentimes this is combined with a point-of-view shot so that the character seeing everything from below feels small, intimidated, frightened, or overpowered. Sometimes, as in *April Fools'* low angle of a New York skyscraper, it suggests power, importance, and coldness. It can be employed in mysteries or thrillers to confer an ominous quality to whatever it is that the character is looking up at. It is also often used to get a child's (and sometimes a small animal's) perspective in a scene.

High-Angle Shot: The reverse of the low-angle shot. The camera is tilted down on what's being photographed. Here too, the psychological implications are reversed. In *The Maltese Falcon* Sidney Greenstreet's character, a huge intimidating fat man, looks down on all he sees. If your character is powerful or haughty or holds himself above the masses, this may be a good angle to occasionally employ—it magnifies the character's importance.

Insert Shot: This is used when we need to see something that is or will be important to the story. The most common example is a clock face. If your characters must synchronize their watches, then often an insert of a watch face—it fills the screen—is included. If a character finds an object, say like a bracelet, and realizes that it's the one that was stolen earlier, an insert shot is used to reveal to the audience that this is the same bracelet. Insert shots are so called because they can be photographed by the second unit and inserted into the film in the editing room.

Now that you've reviewed the definitions of the various shots and their emotional and psychological implications, keep in mind that scripts sometimes use a shorthand. Instead of writing out the shot names, especially when using the mediums, the two-shots, and the full and long shots, often the writer will simply put "ANOTHER ANGLE" or "ANGLE ON" followed by what the camera will focus on. This indicates a shift in the scene and at the same time allows the director of photography to employ his skills and art to determine the particular shot for this scene.

Camera Movement

It's to your advantage to understand the different terms used for shooting when it involves camera movement.

Aerial Shot: This is an exterior shot taken from a plane or a helicopter. If you want the audience to feel the vastness of the landscape or see a large piece of action at once, use this shot. In *The Fugitive* after Kimble has stolen the ambulance, Gerard pursues him in a helicopter and we watch the whole thing, cutting between the aerial shots from above and Kimble's point-of-view shots from the ambulance.

Crane Shot: The camera is put on a special movable crane. From this vantage point it can follow the action's various directions. In *The Wild Bunch* the shoot-out between the bunch and the railroad officials included crane shots.

Dolly, Tracking, Trucking Shots: In these shots the camera either moves alongside the subject of the scene, moves toward or away from the subject, or moves along with the subject as the character walks toward or away from the camera. The shots can be taken from a vehicle (a car, truck, train, etc.) or from tracks (laid down by the grips) on which the camera is mounted. Many times this kind of shot is assumed. For example, if you have two characters walking down a street talking to each other, tracking is implied and noting the type of shot to be done isn't necessary.

With the development of the Steadicam, a scene can be captured without the jiggle or shakiness previously associated with hand-held cameras. The Steadicam thus becomes another means for executing tracking or dolly shots. The camera, hydraulically steadied, is strapped to the cameraman who then follows next to, behind, or in front of the characters who are the focus of the scene. It's great for foot-chase scenes, especially when the chase takes place in a crowd.

Pullback Dolly: This is a camera movement shot that is used to reveal something to the audience that was previously off-screen. It's often used in thrillers or mysteries. The character on screen sees something important off-screen. It's only after the character reacts to it that the camera pulls back and the audience gets to see what the character saw.

Pan, Panning Shot: The pan is short for panorama. In this shot the camera moves horizontally from left to right or right to left around the vertical axis. It's often used in establishing shots. Remember *Patton*? There are about a million pan shots in that film. This shot goes with epic films like vermouth goes with gin.

Swish Pan: This shot is also called a "flash" or "zip pan." It is also a horizontal movement, sometimes 360 degrees, around a vertical axis at such a high rate of speed that the picture becomes a blur. Watch *Snake Eyes* for example. If you watch one of these shots for too long you get dizzy and start wishing the filmmaker could come up with something more sensible.

Thank God the shots are usually of very short duration. When they end, the story often has shifted to a new location.

Tilt Shot: This shot is the vertical version of the pan shot. In this shot the camera moves up and down on a horizontal axis. This shot isn't used as often as the pan, but it has its place. In *Weird Science* the nerds ogle the dream woman they've created with a tilt shot starting at her feet and moving up her entire body.

Through the Lens

A third way to insure that your vision is conveyed more precisely to a film crew, thus enabling you to get one step closer to seeing your vision on screen, involves manipulating the camera lens.

Fish-Eye Lens: There's a very good chance you will never use this particular designation in your script. Basically, it's an extremely wide-angle lens that distorts the image so severely that it appears curved. Only if your characters are on drugs, drunk, or mentally disturbed might you use this. Or if you're doing a music video.

Freeze Frame: A single frame of film is reprinted a number of times so that when it's projected, the image appears to be a still photograph. It's often used at the end of films behind the credit roll.

Rack Focus: If you've ever seen a shot in a movie in which the foreground is in focus and the background is out of focus, or a face on one side of the screen is in focus while the face on the other side of the screen isn't, then you've experienced rack focus. A writer might call for rack focus if something on screen needs to be emphasized, after which the audience's focus needs to be redirected to another part of the screen.

Soft Focus: No, we're not talking about Lucille Ball's close-ups in *Mame*. But it's close. Soft focus is the blurring of everything in the scene except the object of the shot or one plane in the depth of field.

Split Screen: In earlier times if two characters spoke by phone on screen, the filmmakers oftentimes opted to show both characters by using the split screen. If you've ever killed a Saturday afternoon by watching *Pillow Talk* on one of the old movie channels, you saw the split screen technique several times. *The Thomas Crown Affair* (1968) gained a bit of critical notice for its playful (or irritating) use of this technique. It's not seen much these days, but if the hot techniques of the 1960s ever make a comeback, then you'll want to include this approach in your script. Heck, it might be fun to include it in that cutting edge project you're working on this very minute.

Zoom Shot: If you've watched television in the last twenty years, or bought a camera in the last few years, you're already familiar with zooming in or zooming out of scenes. The lens has variable focus lengths and without moving the camera, we can get closer to the action by zooming in on the scene and then move away from it by zooming back out. Use it sparingly in script writing.

Sounds Like

There may be times when you need to indicate how the sound works with what the audience sees on screen. You'll want to indicate this in your screenplay, so you better have the vocabulary. Use these sparingly and have good dramatic justification for their inclusion.

M.O.S: This is one of those famous abbreviations that almost everyone knows. MOS are the initials of "mit out sound," a kind of mangled combination of German and English. It means without sound. If you want one of your scenes to play completely silent, then you need to indicate on the script that it is an MOS scene.

Off-Screen: Always shown as "O.S." If you have a character who is in the scene but is not on screen you use "(O.S.)" for his dialogue. For example, if you have one character in the living room talking to another who is in the kitchen or bedroom you add the "(O.S.)" following the off-screen character's name above his dialogue.

Sound Effects: This is sound, such as window glass being smashed, fire engine sirens, and such added to the film after the shooting is done. It's usually indicated by capitalizing the sound effects you need in a scene. For example:

```
INT. FARM HOUSE - DAY
```

```
Jimmy comes through the screen door, letting it SLAM behind him.
Fluffy awakens at the sound and MEOWS for milk.
```

If you've written a scene in which lots of sounds are heard simultaneously, you might want to note it in the easiest possible way, such as: Appropriate SFX for Times Square on New Year's Eve.

Synchronous and Nonsynchronous Sound: Synchronous means that the image and sound are recorded simultaneously, or appears to be. The sound matches the action on screen. Nonsynchronous is, guess what? Music is often nonsynchronous. But you don't indicate background music by using the above term. You just indicate the music you want behind the action and/or dialogue you've written. Synchronous sound is implied and needs no notation.

Voice Over: The proper way to indicate you're using a narrator for a scene is by capitalizing the character's name and following it with "(V.O.)" above the voice-over dialogue.

Now then, if you go back through your script and add the notations we've just covered where appropriate, the scenes that you've pulled from your head and put on the page will be one step closer to being realized on screen.

CHAPTER NINE

Let the Computer Do It

The computer. Only if you've been in a coma for the past fifteen years could you have missed this addition to the inventory of tools we humans have developed since we slithered out of the water or, depending on your view of human history, Eve lusted after that luscious fruit (before it was a logo).

Computerphobe or computer fan, you can't avoid these machines. Writers who have managed to break off ties with their old IBM Selectric or Royal manual know there's nothing better for an author than these oatmeal-colored gadgets and wonder how they ever got along without them.

Scriptwriting is easier than ever. If you're tired of repaginating every time you make a change or you hate manually formatting and reformatting dialogue you've written, then you must see about buying a scriptwriting program.

Writing software falls into two main categories, those that lead writers through the steps of creating solid stories and characters, and those that format the script properly as you write it. Writers who have used software develop a favorite, and when you try a couple—you can download several demos from the Net—you will too.

There are lots of scriptwriting programs. The following examines the major ones that have been around awhile and have lots of fans among writers. Like all software, of course, they get updated and improved. Let's begin with the story aids.

The first category of software helps writers develop their stories by helping them focus on and analyze story elements and by helping them organize their material. Most programs base their story approach on the three-act structure of Aristotle, Lajos Egri, and Syd Field; on Joseph Campbell's Hero's Journey; or a combination of the two with added touches.

Dramatica Pro is the big guy on the block and has received much praise. It consists essentially of a series of questions that help you define, develop, expand upon, clarify, and refine your story. With the Story Guide, the writer can chose from two categories of questions: the Quick Start, which includes fifty questions and takes three to four hours to complete, and the advanced level which provides two hundred fifty questions and takes a minimum of three or four days to finish.

Questions on both levels are grouped into four topics: setting the stage, story forming, story encoding, and story weaving. Setting the stage includes writing a summary of your idea, choosing a title, and such basic info as that. The second level concentrates on structure, the third on developing the story and fleshing out the skeletal beginnings. The final stage, story weaving, focuses on ways to tell the story whose elements you have now detailed. You can use the program to develop both new and existing stories. You can also apply the information you compile to novels.

This program will make you work (there are no true/false or fill-in-the-blank questions) and it will take you a bit of time to learn, but it can be worth it to get your complete story laid out before you type "FADE IN."

StoryBuilder is simpler than Dramatica. Once loaded it consists essentially of a window with a menu that, in addition to the usual file, edit, and help, includes story, problems, character, setting, plot, and tools. When you select any of these choices, a window pops up with index cards that are to be filled in. For example, under "character," you start with role and after you've given the character a name, you can move on to the character's appearance, inner traits, work, habits, psychological profile, social profile, abilities and skills, likes and dislikes, and backstory. Under the role card there are choices, if you're not sure what role you want your newly created character to play. It can be anything, but the program will suggest protagonist, antagonist, supporting, etc.

With every aspect of your story you can fill out index cards and the computer will save this material until you get it all compiled. It also can suggest story types and stock scenes, and similar organizing material.

This program can help you define and develop your story. But when you get it all together, don't forget you actually have to write it.

Story Craft is even simpler than the previous two programs. It uses what they call the Jarvis Method, named after John Jarvis. Story Craft and Jarvis surveyed the various story-writing methods including Joseph Campbell's Hero's Journey approach, Sid Field's three-act approach, and a couple of others. Jarvis contends that every good story consists of five elements. His twelve-step program will help you form a complete script that includes the five elements. The program doesn't lead the writer through each section with category specific questions; Story Craft is more like a text on computer. You read through a section, then complete that section on your own.

There are also a few other story-building programs you might want to test drive. Writer's Blocks, Write Pro, and Write a Blockbuster also aid the writer in formulating his story.

On the other hand, the formatting programs won't build stories, but they will ease the typing task you face when putting your creation on paper. There are several worth considering.

Final Draft comes with a slightly more intimidating instruction manual than the other programs, but it's very user friendly and isn't written in techno-geek speak. This program offers lots of features and refinements. Go through the tutorial in the book and follow along. You can get the basics, the tab and enter, pretty quickly, then you can move on to learning the additional options. Final Draft offers a great thesaurus and dictionary.

Hollywood Screenwriter is another easily understandable format program that takes little time to get comfortable with. It won't finish typing it for you, and it doesn't have index cards, but it will ease the job of putting your material on the page.

Movie Magic is easy to use and doesn't take much time to get used to. It keeps track of all characters and other elements, such as a setting, you've written so that the second time you refer to it the information is automatically typed. It also features an index card page. Here you can see your scenes in various configurations—nine cards at a time, six, or four. It includes formats for film, television, or stage.

Script Thing is much like Movie Magic—their tutorials both include the "Larry in the Cabin" script—and many of their keystrokes work the same way. Consequently, it's as easy and handy to use. The manual is one of those little spiral-bound books that doesn't overwhelm you at first glance and, from the title on, there's a playful feel to it.

Scriptware has a great reputation because of its ease of use and maybe because of those little icons you can create for each character in your story. Like most of the other programs, this one also anticipates what it thinks you want to type next and utilizes the enter and tab keys. One good thing about this program is that it lets you keep your fingers on the keys almost all the time.

ScriptWizard offers one of the widest varieties of formats of any of the programs. Besides feature-film formatting, it includes stage play, sitcom, radio, and others. If you get the prewritten macros it makes it much easier for those of us who can never remember what that term means. Once you get by some of that stuff it's as easy to use as the others.

All of the above programs are offered in Windows as well as Mac and range in price from around $150 to $350. Every writer will find something to like in all of these packages. Determining which one works best for you will require that you work through the demos so you can get the feel of them. Lots of other kinds of programs can also be found including one called Comedy Writer which is an aid for you know who. There's also a program called Fiction Master, for novelists and short-story writers; IdeaFisher, which helps you brainstorm; and Plots Unlimited. With all these it seems our work is done for us. But no such luck. All that thinking and writing is still up to us; this software just helps focus it all and reduces the time we spend correcting our typos.

If your town or neighborhood computer store doesn't carry the preceding material, try the store that has it all:

- The Writers' Computer Store, 11317 Santa Monica Blvd., Los Angeles, CA 90025; Tel. (310) 479-7774; Web site: *http://writerscomputer.com*

This store carries programs relating to writing and movie-making in general, i.e., budgeting, scheduling, and sample contracts (plus some fun games, but we're trying to be serious here). They also have a very helpful and knowledgeable staff to help you decide what would be best for your needs.

The Web Net

The computer is a gem for writers for yet another reason. Since the development of the World Wide Web in the early nineties, dozens, hundreds, even thousands of companies have opened up web pages. There are so many Web sites devoted to entertainment that it would be impossible to list them all. But, as a writer, you should know that there are usable sites that can be very helpful and informative to you. You might want to check them out, at least once. And, if you're not on the Net, you'll probably want to be after you find out what's available out there.

Let's start with the sites that are specifically focused on Screenwriters.

One place to start is at either *www.wga.org* or *www.wga.org/writtenby/index.html*. This is the site of the Writers Guild and their magazine, *Written By*. You'll find a lot of Guild material here directed specifically at writers and the issues they face writing and selling scripts. This page also provides links to writers' software programs. You're sure to find something here.

Drew's Script-O-Rama can deliver just about any film or television script you might want. Punch the keys and in seconds the script is before your eyes. The screenplays aren't in format, but that shouldn't bother you. They are the same in every other way.

In addition to scripts, this site has most of the features other companies have: chat rooms, contests, a little news, and things like that. Reach them at: *www.script-o-rama.com*.

Story planners, scripts, format information, plot brainstorming, and story planner software demos are all included at the Scriptdude Web page. If you're looking to preview a script writing program, this spot can be helpful. Set your search for *www.scriptdude.com/index.html*.

Getting lots of links to software for writers is one of the payoffs for visiting the Web page called Screenwriters Utopia. To reach them, input *www.screenwritersutopia.com*.

Page is the Professional Authors Group Enterprise bulletin board. Professional writers run this site and you need to prove you are one and pay $50 annually to take part in their news, discussion groups, and other offerings. You can prove you're a pro if you are a member of the Writers Guild, can supply a copy of the cover of your fiction or nonfiction book, can provide an ample number of newspaper or magazine clips (from recognized publications), or are a playwright with membership in the Dramatists Guild or PEN. Their site can be found at *www.pagebbs.com/*.

The Hollywood Writers Network might be of use to you. It's worth checking out. They provide lots of information and links to other writerly sites. Included here are features, directories, and some of the scriptwriting competitions. The address is: *www.hollywoodnetwork.com*.

And, if you've lost your copy of Strunk and White's *Elements of Style,* you might check out Professor Webster's *webster.commnet.edu/Hp/pages/darling/original.htm*. It's all about proper grammar and punctuation.

Another place you will find material you can use is *www.wordplayer.com*. Included are samples of writers' contracts, scripts, and other good stuff.

Other Notable Web Spots

Beyond the sites devoted exclusively to screenwriting or screenplays, there are other sites that can supply you with helpful information about films and the business of making movies.

The dull sounding Internet Movie Database (IMDb) has a very complete inventory of information on thousands of films. Want to know who released a particular film? It's there. Want a list of credits for a particular film? It's there. Want to know how much money a film made? It's there. This place is a real fount of down-to-earth solid information. There's even a page of gossip and goofs for every film. Their address is *http://us.imdb.com/*.

If your local bookstore doesn't carry the *Hollywood Creative Directory* and you think it's a must-buy source of information, you can log on to the directory's site, subscribe, and enjoy the online version of it. Access for this directory, which is updated three times per year, is only $99 a year. You'll find it at *www.hcdonline.com*.

Another page that offers solid information on movies is the Box Office Guru. Here you'll find all sorts of statistics about the movies made since 1989. Don't look for gossip here. Find them at *www.boxofficeguru.com/*.

A less formal approach to movie information can be found at Ain't It Cool News. Here you can find out about movies from pre- through post-production. This isn't the spot for gossip either. So if you want to know how the set-side romances of a particular movie heated up during production, you won't find it here. Ain't that cool? They can be found at, no surprise, *www.aint-it-cool-news.com*.

If you're looking for straightforward news of the industry, you can find it at either *www.variety.com* or *www.hollywoodreporter.com*. These are the

Web versions of the daily trade newspapers. If you want the complete version, you have to subscribe on line, but there's lots of stuff that's free to read, like the box-office results.

Hollywood Online at *www.hollywood.com* offers a movie guide, a studio store, show times for theaters in your area, and information like listings of all the songs from particular films and their box-office results. They also feature movie talk and movie people.

If you can't get enough of general-entertainment news and gossip and you're looking for more than just solid facts and figures, you'll find plenty at several sites. A couple of prominent ones are Entertainment Asylum (*www.asylum.com*) and E! Online (*www.eonline.com*), which is the online version of the Entertainment cable channel. All the celebrity news you could ever want can be found here.

Of even broader scope is Geocities' site. They seem to have something for everyone. Film lovers can punch in *www.geocities.com/Hollywood/*.

The studios haven't let this particular technology pass them by. All of them are represented on the Web. Naturally they provide a menu of all their various business lines, information about their latest offerings, products you can buy, and miscellaneous other information. Most upcoming film releases also establish their own Web page. Check them by name followed by ".com".

If your trips to your local video store to buy a movie or two are unfulfilling, you can always try Spree Movies. They offer thousands of movies on tape as well as books and other offerings such as a gift shop, flowers, coffee, and tea. You can find them at *www.spree.com*.

A particularly interesting Web site is called Access to Hollywood (*www.accesstohollywood.com*). Although Access isn't seeking writers, it is seeking material. They offer a Five Minute Film School in which they give you the basics of becoming a producer by finding material such as unusual out-of-the-way stories, books, or movies. They tell you how to obtain the rights to the material and how to present it to them. If they can sell the idea to a Hollywood production company or studio, you get cut in for some producer's money. It's an interesting concept, but you have to remember, they don't want a pitch for an original story you scripted.

Keep in mind that Web sites are popping up every day, so by the time this is in print, there'll be even more screenwriting spots to check out. If you want to passively slip around the Net, you can, of course, hit the entertainment link on the homepage provided by your particular Internet connection or get Yahoo! (*www.yahoo.com*) to find something about movies for you. But, the above Web pages will focus your search on things you can really use.

See how easy that is? And you were afraid if it involved computers it would be needlessly complicated. It's amazing what can be done when computer geeks work with entertainment types.

CHAPTER TEN

Working Through It

People who don't write or have never been around working writers often think that once writers get an idea they just sit down and start typing it onto the page, stopping only if they can't think of the word they want to use, or hesitating after a sentence here and there to catch their breath.

More sophisticated people know that writers are required to think about what they're going to write, plan it, and make dozens of notes as ideas occur to them.

It's only writers, like you, who know all the goblins that come creeping out to haunt you when you sit down to write. Without warning they just appear, often paralyzing your typing fingers or creating havoc with the wiring in your imagination.

Among the goblins that arrive at your desk ahead of you are the spirits of the material itself. They roost on your monitor and bedevil you with doubt and story problems.

Act two is one of the places where goblins get pretty rowdy. You got act one. You got the story set up, introduced the hero, came to the inciting incident that launched the story, and wrote with ease through the climax of this act. Now you're in act two and the material's getting thinner and thinner. What are you going to do until you get to the climax? Act two sinks many a writer. It's the tough one to write. It's the act that develops character and plot, complicates everything, lets us see some of the stuff under the surface, takes a peek here and there, and sets us up for act three and the big finale.

If this is the sprite that's pinned you down, get to your outline immediately and beef it up. Movies don't go directly from opening to climax. So, if that's as far as you've gotten in developing your screenplay, then you still have a piece of work to do. Instead of sitting at the computer hoping the yellow brick road to act three will magically materialize, you better start paving it instead.

Here's a typical scenario: A teenager's family moves to a new town and he has to enroll at a new high school. You know how to set all this up in act one, and maybe you've planned to have the climax of the first act be the boy's encounter with his antagonist. Act two will focus on the boy realizing what he has to do to achieve his goals that were set up in act one.

You've probably already decided where you want the boy to be by the final page. There are a dozen goals that he can pursue in this particular overworked concept. Is the boy looking for acceptance? Learning a new teen culture? Getting the girl he wants? Beating the school bully? Exposing the school punks as dope pushers? Making the team? Passing the math test and getting accepted at a good college?

This is where the hard work comes in. If you can't get through act two with this material, you probably haven't developed it thoroughly. First, examine all the possible complications that could occur to the boy as he pursues his quest. Make a list of all the things that could or might happen. If, for example, the boy is trying to achieve acceptance at this new school, what might prevent that? What might aid that? The growing conflict in each act isn't a simple arc, positive and negative events happen to push the characters toward the climax. Where does the boy go for solace during his fight? Do you have a character that fulfills that need? How could the subplot work into the primary plot?

Maybe you've omitted a couple of subplots altogether and that's what act two lacks. Perhaps you have a story about three young kids who get lost in the desert or inside a computer-generated virtual reality. You've got plenty of complications to involve the kids, but after you've written four of them, it's getting repetitive and you're only on page sixty-five. Consider developing subplots. In our first story idea, there are lots of subplot possibilities. For example, what about the boy's relationship with his parents? What about their problems in this new town with new jobs? What does the boy do when he's not at school? What about the antagonist's activities? What about positive things the boy discovers as he marches toward his goal?

In *Honey I Shrunk the Kids* the main plot concerned the parents' frantic efforts to find their children. The kids finding their way home served as the major subplot. The children's efforts to get discovered by their dad could have gotten repetitive, but they had a variety of experiences, and a couple of minor subplots focused on the relationships among them.

In the second act let the audience get to know the protagonist a little better. Think of the last half-dozen films you've seen. It's generally in act two that the hero finally beds, or at least falls for, the love interest. And, it's usually in this act that we get to know the personal side of the hero. We might see his other relationships or we learn what he's really interested in pursuing after he dispatches the bad guys.

If act two is getting to you, sit down and rework, enlarge, and refine your outline. It will give you some guidance. Remember, though, don't pad it. The audience will know immediately that the plot's going nowhere and that those long-winded conversations you've included will have no effect on anything in the story. Strive to write tight. Keep anything extraneous, any irrelevant fluff, out of your work. Tight scripts are the ones analysts can't put down.

Other Goblins

It isn't just act two that can get you down and keep you from finishing. And it isn't always the material itself. Sometimes it's what happens when you write. Other goblins plague you. They pop out and sit on your shoulder. They create such a racket it's almost impossible to write. It's no wonder lots of writers take to drinking.

You become unsure of everything you put on the page. You thought it was a great idea when it came to you. You loved it when you rolled it around in your head. You felt clever when you worked out the story. But now a creeping discontent, an unnamed worry, is making its way across your neural synapses. Every word you write seems like the worst choice imaginable. The plot points you developed sit on the page as the least intriguing choices possible. You describe your characters and the words sneer at you. You wish you had paid more attention to that teacher who encouraged you to build your vocabulary. How could you fall so short of your own expectations?

You come to the conclusion that this story is the stupidest idea ever conceived. You visualize what will happen if you give it to any of your friends to read. They'll all meet up at the local hangout and spend the evening laughing their heads off at your ridiculous idea, your terrible writing, and your completely incomprehensible characters. You can't even let yourself imagine what an agent and his assistants will do.

You decide that the whole project, idea and execution, is the worst thing ever brought forth from any currently functioning imagination. You wonder whether or not to shred the whole thing and look for work laying cable or cleaning motel rooms. Good, honest, physical labor has its blessings. One of them is the absence of self-doubt. It's not something you'll achieve as a writer; only the mediocre are satisfied with what they write.

If you don't dispose of your script, you wonder if there's anything worth salvaging in it. You wish you could go back to the day you loved this idea. It's like falling in love. At the beginning it's new and heady. But now that you're getting to know your lover, serious doubts are creeping in.

Where do you go when these gremlins dance with wild abandon on your head? Bypass all the psychologizing handed down from the psychiatrists of the early part of our century and all the pop-psycho-babble of the latter part. Sit down at your word processor. Let the little devils have their say for about ten or twenty minutes while you play hearts or solitaire or type repeatedly "All work and no play make Johnny a dull boy." Then tell them to go to hell; swallow hard and press on, promising yourself a complete and thorough rewrite of this dreck when you reach the final page.

It's almost inevitable that your feelings will change again before you get to the end of your script. And there's a good chance you'll feel better about the material later.

No Finish Line

Have you met people who have never finished their doctoral dissertation? Or people who dropped out of high school just weeks before graduation? Or students who drop out of med school before they finish?

There's just something about finishing. We all live on dreams. But once you finish a script, polish it up, and dress it up for public presentation, the dream is laid to rest, replaced with cold reality. Not only have you translated your imaginings to paper, for all the pain and pleasure that entailed, but now the story is no longer your private domain. It will hardly belong to you at all. You'll get unwanted and unsought comments. You'll peddle it to all kinds of people, and they'll all want to change it—a little or a lot. Your secret pleasure is gone and it can never be exclusive to you again.

So lots of writers just don't finish. They get into it maybe sixty or eighty pages and simply can't get themselves to continue despite having act two worked out. One way to handle this impasse is to put the thing away for awhile. Later, after you've emotionally separated from it, you can go back and take a fresh view of it. If you still like it enough to devote some more time to it, you'll probably be able to finish it with clear-eyed dispassion. Now you will be writing to get it done. On the other hand you might pick it up at a later time and realize it isn't worth finishing. This script was a learning exercise. It served its purpose in your development as a writer. There's no need to finish it. Put it back in the bottom drawer. When you become rich and successful and studios are clamoring for more material from you, you can pull that one out, give it an ending and go on with your next project.

Skinny Devils

A third kind of devil that occasionally haunts writers is in many ways the most fearsome. Occasionally you get deep into your material and you find it's running thin. You've reworked the outline and you've added material, yet it seems to be petering out faster than you can keep it alive.

Just as college freshmen plan to discuss the decline and fall of the Roman Empire in an eight-page paper, writers sometimes try the opposite approach. They think their sensible little story will consume 120 pages. You've probably seen movies, often based on television series, which are criticized for being short on plot. The writers of thirty-minute stories can't, according to the critics, conceive a story that has enough plot to last 110–120 minutes. Sometimes plot-bare movies are referred to as one-joke stories. Remember *Blind Date*? It had one joke, and it was an old one at that. So, there will be times, despite writing careful outlines and taking mental vacations, when nothing you do makes your idea work as a full-length feature film, or an hour-long television series episode. You've run it out. There's not much you can do but set it aside. Maybe sometime in the future you'll have an epiphany and instantly know how to rework the story. Then again, unless you want to try a script consultant, maybe this project will just have to collect dust until the pages crackle and fall away.

Not to worry. You'll fall in love with another idea very soon and be off on a new adventure.

CHAPTER ELEVEN

Finishing Up

Well, here you are. You're finished. It's been ten days, two months, or three years and you've finished your first screenplay.

Congratulations! You completed a big job. You achieved an estimable goal. There were times when you thought you'd never finish and times you wondered whether you should bother. But now it's done.

You should kick back for, at the very minimum, a few days before you look at your work again. Let it cool. It will help you be more objective when you go back to it. And you will go back to it. Even if at this moment you can't bear to look at it. You've lived it and breathed it and rolled around in it for a long time and now you want and need a break. Take it.

The script will call you soon enough and demand to be dealt with again. It's a good thing it will because you aren't finished with it yet. Even if you think you are. You aren't. You just finished one of the two most significant steps of a multistep process.

Taking Another Hard Look

After a week or two or three, or maybe even more, go back to your desk and take out your opus. It's time to get the thing in fighting shape.

Read through it slowly and carefully. You need to see how it feels to you. Does it sound like what you had in mind when you first started on this story? Does the story flow as you had imagined it would? Does it seem sluggish, slow, senseless, confusing, confined, and superficial, or are you still in love with everything you wrote, down to each period and dialogue beginning with "well"? If you still love it all, maybe you need to give it more time to rest. If you can see nothing that needs improving, maybe what you need is another point of view. That will come inevitably, after the first major revision.

Get It Off Your Chest then Off the Page

If this is your first script and your first serious, extensive writing project, there is a good chance you took this opportunity to get everything that was on your chest, in your mind, and weighing on your heart down on paper. In fact, wanting to express all your thoughts is a strong motivating force to work through a 120-page story.

Now for the bad news. As the first step in rewriting your work, you have to excise all your personal grumblings. One sure sign of a first-timer is a script that's more political, philosophical, sociological, or religious diatribe than story. When a story's characters are nothing more than mouthpieces for the author's point of view, a script's in trouble.

Does that mean that movies shouldn't take a particular political stance? Absolutely not. Open the newspaper to the movie/television section and you'll see writers' ideas about life spread all over. If you ever saw the films *Johnny Got His Gun* or *M*A*S*H*, then you've seen writers who have filled stories with their antiwar sentiments. However, they told us stories with characters that behaved as we might expect ordinary people to behave. The stories revolved around people who had to deal with the results of war. In one case it was a tragic story, in the other, comic. If these scripts had had characters lecturing each other, or had they lectured the audience about the evils of war, they wouldn't have made the powerful statements they did.

Oftentimes the television series *Designing Women* and *Northern Exposure* exposed the points of view of the writers. But they entertained us all the while. If this is how you've handled your thoughts about life, that's a fabulous achievement for a first script. In my experience first-timers need to get all that stuff off their minds, then go back through the work and dump most of it out. Incorporate the rest within the context of the main story, and get on with refining it.

Cut It and Clean It, Again

Vladimir Nabokov once said that he rewrote every word he had ever written. Ernest Hemingway, more earthy, said, "The first draft of anything is shit." Of course, not all writers rewrite everything, but rewriting is a part of the job. Nine chances out of ten your work will be improved by rewriting it at least, at the very least, once.

So, after you scrape off the excessive philosophical musings and disgruntled ravings, face your story squarely and determine that you're going to shape it up. Determine what must go. Look at the length of your screenplay. If you're over 120 to 125 pages, you most certainly must cut. And you can. You may not think so at first, but you can. Go back through all your descriptions. Cut them down. We'll understand what you are describing even if you use three, six, or twenty fewer words to tell us about it. More importantly, go back through the dialogue. You will probably find that you've repeated yourself and explained too much in your characters' speeches. It can be cut. Get your characters' dialogue down to three or four lines and, in some cases, less. Check the script for typos and grammatical errors. If you feel unsure of yourself in this area, get to the bookstore and buy a copy of Strunk and White's *Elements of Style;* it's been the authority on good writing forever. Fix all that you find. There will be others you miss. Most importantly, the first page must be *flawless,* absolutely flawless. It's the first-impression page. If it is sloppy, error-ridden, or placed on the page incorrectly, the analyst, the producer, and the reader—any reader—will despair.

After you've finished the obvious things, go back through and rethink your story. Is it excessively straightforward? Think of how you can take some unexpected detours and still find your way home by fade out. Does it flow logically? Does it make any sense? Is it interesting? Have we seen stories very similar to yours on TV about a thousand times? What makes yours different? Anything? If not, give it something different. Do you have any subplots? How do they work with the primary plot? Are your act climaxes clear, do they turn the story?

Now take a look at your characters and give each of them a grilling. At each stage in the story, in each scene in which a character is faced with alternative choices, why does the character make the decision he or she makes? What other decisions might the character make? You need to go back and get to know your characters again. They don't just exist to make your plot work. You can't have them running hither and yon just because the plot demands it. They have rights, they have personalities, and they often have minds of their own. They'll help you write, or in this case re-write, your script if you give them a little freedom. Once you really get to know them, you'll probably want to change more dialogue, only this time it will be change that flows out of the character's personality.

You may rewrite two, three, or more times, plus do some tweaking here and there. You'll probably know when you're done, when it feels complete. If you ignore this feeling and keep playing with it, it might be because you fear the next step in the process.

Go Public

Move into the next phase slyly and obliquely by first fixing the format one last time. When you are completely finished set it on your desk and gaze upon your baby with pride. It's all dressed up and ready to go. It needs to be at its best. The next steps are difficult ones. Not every writer chooses to do this, but many do, and it can be very helpful to new writers. Ask someone to read it.

Start easy here. Ask a friend. A friend probably can't give you any professional criticism (unless your friend happens to be William Goldman or Linda Seger), but by starting out asking a good friend, you have time to get used to the idea of someone reading your words. And when your friend reports back to you, listen between the lines. If they say they missed something early on and so didn't understand something at the end, or if they really hated a character you meant to be likable, then you've got some criticism without your friend knowing he or she helped you.

If you're in a writing group ask one of them to read your work. They can give you new insights to the story. So far you've controlled the universe you created on paper and things have worked pretty much the way you said. But another reader coming from a whole different sensibility can see your work in a light you never considered. That alternative outlook can help strengthen it.

Getting someone with knowledge of screenwriting, storytelling, and character-building will also aid you in your quest to make your work the best it can be. A professional story analyst will cost you a few bucks, but it should be worth it. Analysts who have worked in the film business for some time understand what is required for a screenplay to succeed. There are a couple of considerations here. The analyst should critique your story as a story and also estimate your work's chances of impressing Hollywood. For example, perhaps your screenplay is very familiar; it's a story that's been done to death. But, the analyst knows that there is always a market for this particular kind of material. Further, you've put a fresh twist on it. (Think of all the buddy movies you've seen.) In that case, you have a chance of succeeding.

On the other hand, maybe the analyst will see a story well told, unique, and clever. But Hollywood knows that such stories rarely sell many tickets. So, despite your fine work, you'll really struggle to sell it. The upside is that good writing gets you noticed even if the script that shows it off isn't bought or produced.

After getting the responses of the people you've asked to read your work, you can take their notes and decide which are valid criticisms and which say more about them than they do about your screenplay. For example, maybe a friend will tell you they hated your main character because he was a drunk, or he started out as a drunk and didn't get better. That kind of comment probably says more about your friend and what he is and is not sympathetic to. If you wrote your whole story around a character who's a drunk, that was your intention and this criticism can be taken with a grain of salt. If, however, the reader missed the redemption scene, maybe it wasn't strongly and clearly written. You need to take a look at it.

If you have any contact with theater groups, actors, or even good readers, or if you know a drama teacher who has classes of students who might read your work, it can be an extremely helpful exercise.

Doing a reading or a readers' theater presentation of your work will let you see immediately what dialogue doesn't work, what sings, and what runs counter to the characters you've created. The holes in the plot will glare at you. Remember, when you wrote the material it was just you and your word processor, and you already knew what was going to happen.

If you decide to get people together to perform your work orally, the best of all possible worlds is finding a professional director and actors to perform. Good theater directors can see possibilities in your work that you're probably unaware of. They can bring a fresh approach and new insights to it.

If getting the services of a professional director isn't a possibility, there are other options. If you know someone with directing experience and actors with some experience, it will be to your advantage to ask them to read.

If you're going to rely on giving directions yourself to friends who've agreed to read your work, give them copies ahead of time and encourage them read through it, or at least their lines, several times. A cold reading can do your work a disservice.

Consider asking people you know to attend the reading and listen to the performance. They too can give you helpful feedback.

The Critics

This can all be pretty scary, especially if you're inexperienced. When you write, you lay yourself, or some part of yourself, bare. Every writer experiences it. Committing something to paper, something from your heart, moves you from entertainment consumer to entertainer. Your work is out there for everyone to see and judge.

Any criticism you may get is never easy to take. Even experienced writers struggle with it. You feel at the least a little wounded. That's another reason why it's good to get some distance from your work. When you are on the receiving end of critical analysis, you secretly decide everyone who said anything negative is an insensitive idiot who understands nothing. But deep inside, one of the goblins laughs and tells you you're the idiot.

Give it a little time. Sometimes an hour or two takes off the sting. Sometimes by the next day the criticism looks pretty valid and suddenly you have some new ideas to make this terrific work even better. You're on your way again. After more rewrites you will know when it's time to start showing your baby to possible adopters.

Something to remember: it must be human nature to remember the unkind rather than the complimentary comment. Strive to remember the positive. Both positive and negative are equally valid or invalid, as the case may be. And while you're hurting, remember how much you can learn from the negative responses.

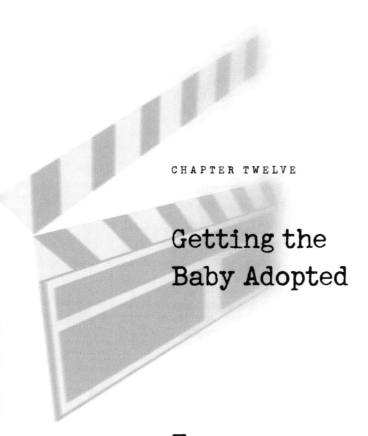

CHAPTER TWELVE

Getting the
Baby Adopted

The writing, rewriting, and testing are done. Your baby's at his best and now you'd like someone to adopt him; someone who will bring the little darling to his full potential.

Before you go any farther, you want to protect junior from the cold, so you'll want to register your screenplay with the Writers Guild. On a cover sheet list the title of the material and your full legal name, social security number, address, and phone number. Attach this sheet to an unbound copy of the script, enclose a check for $20 (for nonmembers), and sent it to:

- WGA Registration, 7000 W. Third Street, Los Angeles, CA 90048; Tel. (323) 782-4500

When the script is received, it is sealed in an envelope, the date is recorded, and a receipt is sent to you that includes a registration number.

How do you get the baby adopted? Move to Los Angeles; get to know some people, and eventually you'll meet someone who knows someone who knows someone to whom you can slip the script. Or move to L.A., get a job at a restaurant where the big producers or the top agents hang out, and slide one of them the script with their double decaf cappuccino.

You probably don't want to do that. You want to stay in Minneapolis or Fort Wayne or Dunwoody. You also want to make the biggest script sell since J. Esterhaus' last deal. It's a very big order.

The Other Half of the Work

You've heard it before, but it bears repeating: writing your script is only half the job. The second half of the job, and by far the harder, is selling it. In the writing stage you are in control. You create a universe and characters and a story that is all your own. But back in this world, which you didn't create, you have to try to convince people who see dozens and dozens of scripts every week that they should take an interest in yours. You have hardly any control at all.

To help you with the adoption, excluding a change of address, your next best bet is to make an extended trip to Los Angeles. If you can swing a six-month sabbatical to the entertainment capital, you should do it. Spending time in the city of angels helps because it will:

- Give you a chance to see how the industry works.
- Give you an L.A. address, at least temporarily.
- Provide an opportunity to take advantage of the many programs, classes, presentations, and offerings around town.
- Let you get familiar with the town so it won't seem so foreign later if you need to attend meetings.
- Provide information about the industry, from the *Los Angeles Times* and *Daily Variety* to overhearing your neighbors argue about which one should audition for Mel Gibson's next movie.
- Get you away from all those people at home who keep you from writing.
- Give you the opportunity to meet people in the industry, which may lead to meeting more people in the industry.
- Provide the possibility of doing something really stupid that may catch the eye, ear, attention, or curiosity of someone who then might like to meet the nut and subsequently agree to look at your script.
- Give you the chance to see if all the horror stories you've heard about Los Angeles are true or exaggerated—after all, about fourteen million people live in the L.A. area; there must be something attractive about it.
- Encourage you to diet. You'll notice as you make your way around

the industry and the places where people connect to it that there aren't any fat people. Okay, that's an exaggeration, but take a look when you get there.

- Give you a chance to look at the real estate and pick out the area where you want to live once the script sells. (When you see the prices for homes, you'll understand the high cost of making movies.)

If you aren't convinced you should pack your bags, even for a temporary trip, you can try the following strategies for getting someone to take a look at your work. Even if you do move to the city, you should use these methods as an adjunct to your other efforts.

There are lots and lots and lots of scripts floating around the industry. You have to break through and get yours seen. It takes persistence and toughening up your ego.

If you know no one in the industry, no one at all, try the six degrees of separation approach (let's leave poor Kevin Bacon out of it). Someone you know may know someone who works in or is related to someone in the business in some way. Keep working through those people and eventually you'll introduce yourself to someone in the business, maybe over the telephone. It's okay. Once you've got someone in the business, they will know others. Keep working this line of action until you find someone who can help you get a script in somewhere, or at least until you get to someone whose name you can drop as leverage to permit you to send your material or get through to one of the story people.

In addition to doing the six degrees, get a list of agents and production companies. There are several ways to do this. The Writers Guild publishes a list of agents. For a small sum they will send you the list or you can go online (*www.wga.org*) and see what they have to offer. In addition to this there are several directories of directors, writers, agents, production companies, and others. (See chapters 5 and 9.)

Get these lists and directories. Mark those companies that have produced movies in the same genre and for the same medium as yours. Next to this keep the list of agents (more about them later) you plan to call.

In order to be as smooth as possible on the phone and eliminate stammering and stumbling, create a phone script. First and foremost, your pitch should be delivered with enthusiasm for your project. The feeling among agents and production companies is that if you're not a believer in your work and in yourself, why should they believe in you? After introducing yourself, mention that you think their company might be interested in your material—it's their kind of project. Follow that with a brief two liner about the material, summing it up in its best, sexiest, hippest, most intriguing wrapping. Add a couple of lines about yourself—your experience as a writer and why you're a writer they can believe is serious about succeeding.

If this is the first thing you've ever written and you don't have any professional writing experience, mention the classes and training you've had. If you get a chance you might mention your intimate connection with the topic of your screenplay (if you have one), which may make up for your lack of writing experience. Remind yourself that John Grisham was a lawyer, not a creative writing teacher, before he wrote his first book.

Once your phone script is honed, there's another step to take. Like a corporate public relations person preparing the company president for a public appearance, you should make a Q & A, a list of remarks or questions that you might get from the assistant or agent. Prepare answers to them. The answers should convey that this is material worthy of her consideration and you as a writer are worthy of the name.

Get your names, your phone script and your Q & A and start warming up your dialing finger. Try and forget what your telephone bill will look like at the end of the month.

Talk Is Cheap

When you call you might not get a chance to go through the whole script and you'll have to improvise. There are fairly standard responses you'll probably get.

The assistant may tell you:
- Send a synopsis
- The company isn't looking for material at the present
- They don't accept any material not represented by an agent

The assistant wants to get you off the phone.

If the assistant puts you through to the creative affairs person or a development person, chances are they will tell you the same things the assistant did. If you're lucky enough to get through to one of these people, they will probably be even less interested in having their time wasted, but more interested in an intriguing story. In that oh-so-brief moment you have them on the line, sell your heart out. Every development person is looking for the next great film—if their company can afford to make it and if they think it can make money. One of my students recently used this call-around approach and got two companies to agree to look at his material. One of them, HBO, even returned the message he left.

If you are calling an agent they may tell you:

- They only take writers referred to them by writers they currently represent
- The agency isn't taking on any new clients at the present time
- Send a synopsis and they'll get back to you

If you convince them to let you send a synopsis, make sure you know what length they want. Some companies like one paragraph, others a page or so. Make sure you get the person's name, spelled correctly, to whom you should send the material. Make that paragraph or page the best writing you've ever done in your life. Think of it as a sales pitch, not just a story summary.

Through it all, don't forget to be kind and pleasant to assistants, they can be very helpful and they often have much more influence than you might think. They're in the training seat for becoming a story person or an agent.

If the assistant tells you to have your agent send the material, he may just be trying to get rid of you—assuming you don't have an agent. And you don't. But if you feel strongly that your story is right for this particular company then be persistent. Volunteer to send it with a release form. Ask the assistant what he suggests you do. Your enthusiasm, confidence, and belief will help you overcome some resistance.

Don't let rudeness or brusqueness throw you off track. Just keep going and don't take any of it personally. Think of yourself as an actor with a role to play. That separates it from you and makes it easier.

Mail Is Cheaper

Another way to tackle getting an agent or getting a production company to take a look at your work is to write them a query letter that contains the same material as your phone script. Leave lots of white space on the page and include about two or three short paragraphs about the story and about your background. Put the one-paragraph synopsis on a separate page. Make sure your name is on it and that it is attached to the letter. Send the material to a specific person. Just call the company and ask them to whom the material should be directed. Again, get the correct spelling of the contact name.

When you query companies or agencies, you're not asking permission to send the material, you're just sending it. The downside of using the mail is that letters tend to be easy to overlook and get lost in that large stack of incoming scripts.

It Beats Snail Mail

A third alternative is to send your material by e-mail. A couple of writer friends were successful in getting the opportunity to submit their material through this channel. However, that was a couple of years ago. Now, with so much e-mail flying across the Internet and no sign that it will lessen in the next fifty years, people's mailboxes are full of material they never have time to look at.

But every means, promising and not so promising, should be used, and it doesn't take much time to go online and search out studios and companies. As with the other methods, get the correct spelling of the correct person's name at the company you wish to approach, then e-mail them directly, if possible.

Joining writers groups and taking classes and workshops is another avenue to pursue. Several groups in the Los Angeles area hold seminars and feature industry speakers. You don't have to live in L.A. to belong. And there are regularly published journals that are dedicated to listing synopses of writers' scripts. See chapter 5.

Staying Home

At the beginning of this chapter you were encouraged to get an address in Los Angeles. Okay, there might be some reasons for staying in place. Films about Hollywood and the filmmaking process are rarely successful at the box office. *The Player, The Big Picture,* and *Mistress,* no matter how well done and how well received critically, hold no interest to the average moviegoer. Because of this lack of enthusiasm, Hollywood is usually looking for non-Hollywood, real-life tales. You may have such a story, or two. That's one reason to stay home. Your vision is unpolluted by southern California. If you move to L.A. you slowly (or quickly) get into the lifestyle and before you know it you think Hollywood is the center of the universe. Goodbye interesting stories, hello more of the same. Besides, you've got friends and cheaper rent where you are now. L.A. can be expensive and lonely. There, it's said.

You've got the material. You want to get it out in circulation where someone can see it and give you a chance. It's up to you to make this happen. Even with an agent, you've got to make the calls and hustle for work. So what are you waiting for?

The Agents

You probably already heard the story about agents: you can't get one unless you're already successful. And if you are successful, you already have one.

Getting an agent is no walk on the beach. It takes persistence, something to show them, and a willingness to be treated with less respect than death-row prisoners get. Don't be too hard on agents. Well, you can be a little hard, but give them just the tiniest of breaks. They have a lot of people clambering at their doors. Those clamberers think the agents can do something for them. If they have people soliciting their attention all day long, eventually they may begin to feel that they possess some kind of magic, maybe they get smug and start treating people with the same dignity they usually save for cockroaches. Contrariwise, maybe they just get weary—weary of bad writers, writers who don't learn the business, and writers who think they are the second (first if you're Jewish) coming. Then again, maybe they just need time to do the work that's on their desks before moving on to the next phone call or plea from an unknown.

It may seem like agents mostly go to lunch and schmooze, but they may, in actuality, be working. A lot of their work is schmoozing. Successful agents work for their clients so they don't have much time for untried writers. If you were a current client, would you want your agent wasting time with an unknown instead of negotiating a better deal for you? No, probably not.

Agents know how hard it is to sell the work of new writers. It's a double sell: the script and the script's author. And if the script isn't a high concept work or doesn't have an easily identifiable audience, then the agent has to work doubly, doubly hard. The representative has to convince someone at the studios that the script would make a swell movie, despite the fact that it isn't an action or coming-of-age piece, it isn't a script written for an ex–*Saturday Night Live* comic, and it doesn't feature characters under twenty-five.

As a beginner, how do you deal with this? Besides following all the previous suggestions in this book, you ought to know something about the agencies. Start calling agencies. Ignore most of the advice you get about who does and who doesn't look at new writer's work, and call them. If you can get a bit of your pitch out to just about anyone at the other end and they respond even semifavorably, you've just put your toe in the door—ever so slightly. Later the toe may get slammed on and hurt like hell for a day or so but it may also be the mini-break you've been looking for.

If you really don't have any contacts in the business, you have to be ready for some hard knocks, and playing the percentages is probably better than picking out a couple of agencies and investing all your hopes and dreams in them. Better spread your efforts around at the beginning. Even if you don't have any success, you've got a bit more experience with the telephone script you've written for yourself and you're getting smoother and smoother at it. To give yourself comic relief replay the "Gotta Dance" scene in *Singin' in the Rain*.

The Agency Family Tree

Agencies range from one-person offices to huge conglomerates that represent writers as well as actors, directors, and sometimes other kinds of performers. These places are so potent that they tell the studios what movies to make. That's an exaggeration, but not much of one. As you might have guessed, there is an agency hierarchy from the most prominent and prestigious on down.

There's every chance the largest and most prestigious agency won't take the time to talk to an unrepresented, never-represented, unproduced writer.

If you want to skip them in your search, it will be easier on your ego. But you won't get any practice with your telephone talk.

Among agencies there are the big three. Unlike Detroit they've never lost their market, although they've all had their ups and downs over the years.

First, if you consider yourself a working writer or an aspiring writer, then you must know Creative Artists Agency (CAA). This is the agency that got Coke signed, and finally after years of leading the company, the boss, Michael Ovitz, left to go to Disney (which didn't work out too well). This is one of the agencies that has so much clout, you genuflect when you pass the building.

- Creative Artists Agency (CAA), 9830 Wilshire Blvd., Beverly Hills, CA 90212; Tel. (310) 288-4545

ICM is another acronym you should know. It is short for International Creative Management, which has been around since the early 1970s and has had its good days and bad days. Usually it's fighting with CAA to be considered number one in the hearts (for those who have hearts, that is) of industry people.

- International Creative Management (ICM), 8942 Wilshire Blvd., Beverly Hills, CA 90211; Tel. (310) 550-4000

The final big-three member isn't known by its initials but is generally referred to as William Morris. The agency, the most historic of the three, was founded at the turn of the century. It has almost seen its demise on more than one occasion, most recently in the early 1990s, before they folded-in a successful, smaller agency, Triad, and regained their foothold as one of the essential powers that be.

- William Morris Agency (WMA), 151 El Camino Drive, Beverly Hills, CA 90212; Tel. (310) 274-7451

Although the big three usually don't admit that any smaller houses are significant, they are. The following include the most highly regarded second tier agencies:

- Endeavor, 9701 Wilshire Boulevard, Tenth Floor, Beverly Hills, CA 90212; Tel. (310) 248-2000
- United Talent Agency (UTA), 95160 Wilshire Boulevard, #500, Beverly Hills, CA 90212; Tel. (310) 273-6700

The following include the most highly regarded second tier agencies:

- The Agency, 1800 Avenue of the Stars, #400, Los Angeles, CA 90067; Tel. (310) 551-3000
- The Broder Kurland Webb Uffner Agency, 9242 Beverly Boulevard, #200, Beverly Hills, CA 90210; Tel. (310) 281-3400
- The Gersh Agency, 232 N. Canon Drive, Beverly Hills, CA 90210; Tel. (310) 274-6611
- Paradigm, 10100 Santa Monica Boulevard, Los Angeles, CA 90067; Tel. (310) 277-4400
- Writers and Artists, 924 Westwood Boulevard, #900, Los Angeles, CA 90023; Tel. (310) 824-6300

The following midsized agencies are well established on the playing fields of Hollywood. (That means they've been doing business longer than five years.)

- Agency for the Performing Arts (APA), 9000 Sunset Boulevard, #900, Los Angeles, CA 90069; Tel. (310) 273-0744
- The Artists Agency, 10000 Santa Monica Boulevard, #305, Los Angeles, CA 90067; Tel. (310) 277-7779
- The Gage Group, 9255 Sunset Boulevard, #515, Los Angeles, CA 90069; Tel. (310) 859-8777
- Innovative Artists, 1999 Avenue of the Stars, #2850, Los Angeles, CA 90067; Tel. (310) 553-5200
- Major Clients Agency, 345 Maple Drive, #395, Beverly Hills, CA 90210; Tel. (310) 205-5000
- Jim Preminger Agency, 1650 Westwood Boulevard, #201, Los Angeles, CA 90024; Tel. (310) 475-9491
- Shapiro-Lictman-Stein, 8827 Beverly Boulevard, Los Angeles, CA 90048; Tel. (310) 859-8877

These are the most stable agencies. You'll probably be all right with them, if you can get them to look at your material, but don't consider this list an endorsement of the above and a condemnation of those not included.

The Little Kids on the Block

Your third choice is to go for the smaller boutique agencies. These smaller houses are probably your best bet. It's hard to know, without visiting them personally, how businesslike, how busy, and how reputable they may be. Outside of pretending to be a flower delivery person with the wrong address, it's difficult to simply walk into an agency to take a look around, although you might give it a try.

A more economic approach to cull the wheat from the chaff is to ask around about smaller agencies. Small agencies generally specialize in one medium or the other. You'll need to know this before you approach them. If you take writing classes or attend workshops, other attendees can be valuable sources of information about agents. This kind of gossip can be good. If you have neighbors who work in the business, ask them what they know about any agencies.

If you speak to an agency that isn't taking clients—and you're more likely to have an actual conversation with someone at a small agency—ask them if they know of any agencies that are open to new clients or if they know of any new agencies that are being formed.

A newly formed organization might be the best thing for you. They're hungry to succeed and their client roster isn't yet full—unless the principals came from other agencies and brought every single one of their former clients with them.

Reading the trades can help you with your search. When a new agency forms, it's covered by the journals. When a deal is made, the agent involved is mentioned in the article. Other tidbits can be found throughout the various features that are run each day.

During this fight to be noticed by an agent, it's nice to get some perspective on the problem by remembering that you are hiring someone to do something for you. When you hire a painter or a plumber you look for the best deal for the least money, and you choose. But when it comes to agents, even though they are the vendor, so to speak, you don't get to pick and choose until you are well established and bankable. For now you look for agents, but they are the ones that get to choose.

There's no guarantee that you'll be treated better or worse by large, mid-size, or small agencies. There is a mixture of rudeness and kindness at all levels. A super-small agent may be more willing to listen, but it may be because he has nothing better to do. One thing that is admired in the business is persistence, and when it's perceived, others, including agents, are often willing to help because they admire the drive and are familiar with the struggle for recognition.

There is another alternative. If you're willing to do all the calling, you can get an attorney to represent you. They won't sell your material or schmooze over three-hour lunches, and they may or may not have some possible contacts for you, probably not, but studios and production companies can accept material sent to them by attorneys. If this tactic appeals to you, it's best if you hire an entertainment lawyer who's familiar with writers' contracts.

CHAPTER FOURTEEN

What You Can Expect

You've been on the phone for hours and hours, days and days. You've been treated rudely and not so rudely but finally you got a couple of companies to agree to take a look at your query letter, your synopsis, or your script. In terms of salesmanship, that's not a bad average.

What can you expect now? There are always stories about people who send out a query and two days later make a million dollar deal. This is mostly hype sent out by agents and managers who want to pump up their agency's and the writer's reputation for obvious reasons. It's a rare exception that a query letter gets read immediately and the script follows suit.

Give the query letter or the synopsis about a week, possibly two. Then begin calling the contact person. You probably won't speak directly with her, so leave a message. By calling you may encourage her to read the letter or synopsis if she hasn't yet done so. It will let her know you are concerned, believe in your project, and are following it up. And if you have been lucky enough to get interest from another agent to whom you sent the material, make sure you leave that in the message also. As soon as one agent is interested, others will increase their attention to you.

Script, Script, Who's Got the Script?

There are several things that are possible after you send them material. They can reject it. They can lose it. They can forget they asked for it and you have to remind them of your previous call(s) to bring them up to speed and maybe remail the material. They can ignore all your subsequent follow-up calls. They can disappear. It's very likely that they won't answer any messages you might leave for them. That's the worse case.

The best case is that they like your synopsis and ask to see the script. They'll send a release form. When you receive it, read it, sign it, and make a copy of it. Include a cover letter addressed to the specific person who contacted you. In the first line of the letter tell her you are sending the material at her request. Refer to your material by name and thank her for agreeing to take a look at it. This letter should be kept short repeating only the brief history of why it's coming into the agency. Take the letter and the release, paper clip them to the script and send it to her or deliver it yourself. Make sure it's a *copy* of your script. Find out if she wants a self-addressed envelope included with the script when you send it to her. This time give the agency about three weeks before you start your follow-up.

Several things may happen. You can get the script with a rejection letter before the three weeks have passed. Or very shortly after you call the agency you will get the turndown and the script returned without having spoken to the person who asked for it. More commonly, you will call and be told, by an assistant, that it hasn't yet been read. That can mean it hasn't been read, he can't find it, no one has any memory of your script (another reason to spend some time on your title), or he just doesn't have time to deal with your script now. Tell him when you will call back.

There's not much you can do about any of this. You wait another week and call again. This routine may go on for several weeks. An agent once called me after I had inquired about the status of my script and told me he liked it, but he hadn't yet finished it. He suggested I call back in two weeks. I did. He wasn't in and didn't return my call. Another week. Another call. This time he had no memory of the previous conversation or of the script. I decided that I didn't need a granola brain as my agent.

After looking at the synopsis or the script, they may ask to meet with you. If they don't meet with you they might tell you that they liked the material and they have a couple of places they would like to send it. You say okay and then you wait. You should check up on it at about two- or three-week intervals. Now is the time to get the agent to look at your other material. Don't bombard him, but launch an attack to be noticed. When you were in grade school, who got the attention? The terrors, the whiners, and the charmers. Well?

The Meeting

If the agent asks you to meet with him, you need to get ready. Reread the script if you haven't done so recently. It will be fresh in the agent's mind, and you don't want to be caught not remembering what you wrote.

You're not going into this meetings as next year's Academy Award winner. You're going to pitch, i.e., sell this guy your writing. Take out all your other scripts and review them. The agent will undoubtedly ask you about other writing. Bring copies and pitch them. Get out your idea file or rethink the latest concept that's been keeping you up nights. Be prepared to pitch these also.

The morning of your meeting call the agent's office to reconfirm. Hollywood isn't about taking meetings; it's about rescheduling meetings. Get cleaned up but don't get too formal. Hollywood, at least the creative and production side, is pretty casual.

Your main goal is to listen and be listened to. One of the big challenges in a meeting is to get the agent (or producer or whomever you're seeing) to stop answering the phone. If he is the courteous sort, he will have the calls stopped, if not, you may be talking between rings. This isn't a good thing for you.

This is the time for the agent to get to know you a little and vice versa. He wants to be assured that you are serious about your work and he will probably want to know a little about your past career.

The agent will ask you questions about the script. There will be things in it he doesn't understand, doesn't follow, or doesn't think work. You can point out appropriate character motivations or events that lead from one plot point to another in response to his questions, but don't go overboard.

He may suggest changes. You don't want to be unreasonable, but you shouldn't be too willing to go along with everything he says either. No one admires people who are too weak. A discussion, without rancor, is in order. You have to pick and choose your battles. What changes do you think would really wreck the essential nature of the script? What changes might just make it flow better, or at least wouldn't harm it?

There are no hard and fast rules in all this. It's impossible to predict what the outcome of the meeting might be. If you are meeting with a producer, she may like your writing but not be interested in this particular material. She offers to add your name to her writers' list. The list is used if something comes up and she needs writers. Getting added to a writers' list feels good but doesn't generally result in getting any work.

Of course, if you could come into the meeting with a director and a big-name actor attached to your script, the sailing would be much, much easier. Everyone's interested in a nice neat package that can be set up somewhere.

As one veteran writer, who has written four novels and several plays and has several projects currently making the rounds, said, "I've learned how to do meetings. At SC [University of Southern California] in one class we had to pitch our ideas to each other. If you have the most rudimentary acting skill, you can act your way through it. Or take an acting, improv, or stand-up class. I've had enough failure not to be worried anymore. There's only so much you can control. You take care of that, then relax."

My first agent didn't even call me in. When I called her to check up on the material a week after I gave it to her she said she had read it and was going to submit it to the television series people the next day. It was easy and for awhile it seemed that they might buy it. But, in the end, the production company decided against it. I didn't see my agent face to face and get to know her until I sent her a feature script and took her to lunch to talk about it.

Contract Talks

Whether or not you meet with an agent, the ideal result of getting your stuff to him is for the agent to ask you to sign a contract for the project he read. Among all the small print about you vouching that the material is really your original work and that you have no other people representing it nor is it presently under consideration by any company, is the information that the agency agrees, for a specified period of time, to attempt to sell your work. The agency gets a 10 percent commission for its efforts.

If the agent is really, really crazy about your work, he could ask to see the other scripts you've been bugging him to look at. If he likes those as well, he might want to sign you to an agency contract. Usually, the contracts are for a year or two in length, include all the same material as the other contract, and also specify a 10 percent fee. That's the limit licensed agents can charge. Representing project by project is currently the more common practice among agents.

These agent meetings might be the beginning of a whole new phase of your career or they might just be another meeting. But remember to prepare yourself and have other ideas to pitch. It just may be that the idea you toss out to him as you're walking out the door will pique his interest.

CHAPTER FIFTEEN

Other Options

If your attempts to get an agent or production company to look at your material meet with no success, then consider yourself one of the family. It happens to thousands of writers. It proves nothing about your writing.

Being turned down can signal a dozen different things. It can mean that the agency doesn't represent the kind of work you sent them. It can mean the agency has no good contacts with the television show you wrote a spec episode for. It can mean the agent isn't taking any more clients. It can mean the agent just lost his assistant and doesn't have time to read anything, and it can mean that the month your script came into the agency the agent was in the hospital and simply had to bypass whatever stacked up during that time.

As you already know, and have heard over and over (and that's just in this book), this is a very competitive business. There are so many scripts out there they're like notes in bottles bobbling about a crowded sea searching for someone to pick them up. Agents can't read them all, producers can't read them all, and, in fact, no one can read them all.

Every agent, producer, and studio in town wants to find the next big film—the film that will win an Academy Award, change the way films are made, change Hollywood, or make a whole wad of money, preferably all four. Consequently, those charged with finding scripts would love to have the time to peruse everything that's out there. But it's not possible. Experienced readers who sift through tons of material know that most scripts, while they may be okay or even good, even very good, disqualify themselves for various reasons. Maybe they aren't the kind of material the studio's looking for, maybe the budget is too big for the reader's company, and on and on.

Don't despair or consider yourself a failure. You've got some other avenues to pursue before you take that job selling insurance. You can hang out at Morton's, the new Spago, the Grill, or any of the currently hot places to go and try and meet someone who can help. This approach may or may not work. If you try this approach, remember you have to keep abreast of the in places—they change pretty rapidly in Los Angeles.

There are other means that don't require driving into the city every night and spending big bucks at a bar.

In the past few years a couple of enterprising women have created vehicles in which writers can show their work without first lassoing an agent to do it for them. Natalie Lemberg Rothenberg, a story analyst who has taught classes at The American Film Institute as part of UCLA's extension writing program and at other venues, has a company called the Insiders System for Writers through which she offers two services. She will thoroughly evaluate your material, whether it be a script, play, novel, nonfiction material, or other kinds of writing, and give you eight to ten pages of notes. For this service she charges $275.

The second service she provides is a listing of your script, novel, or nonfiction material in her quarterly publication called *Writers Showcase*. Each script or other material that is included in the publication is given a full page. A log line written by Lemberg Rothenberg, the author's summary of the material, and a box score (similar to those used by the studios) of the various elements of the screenplay including structure, characterization, and such as that are featured on the page. This service goes for $175.

Each issue of *Writers Showcase* features from forty to not-more-than sixty summaries and is distributed to more than 250 agents and producers. Since she began a couple of years ago, over sixty of the writers featured in the magazine have found representation or made deals on their material. To contact Natalie:

- Insiders System for Writers, Natalie Lemberg Rothenberg, 1223 Wilshire Blvd., #336, Santa Monica, CA 90403; Tel. (800) 397-2615; e-mail: *Insiderssystem@msn.com*

The *Spec Script Marketplace* is the brainchild of Eva Peel, another experienced member of the industry. In this publication the boxed entries include the title and a fifty-word blurb. In Eva's words, "It's a log line and a little sizzle, in other words, the equivalent of a thirty-second phone pitch." The listings are anonymous. If any of the twelve hundred to thirteen hundred movie producers, studio executives, and development executives to which she distributes the *Marketplace* are interested, they call her and she passes the information along to the writer. Each listing in the bi-monthly publication costs the writer $39, with $35 for each renewal. To contact Eva:

- *Spec Script Marketplace,* Eva Peel, P.O. Box 1365, Santa Monica, CA 90406; Tel. (310) 396-1662

Another Way to Glory

There's more. Entering screenplay competitions is another means of getting your script seen. Every year there seems to be more of these competitions springing up. They're worth considering.

If you want a complete, updated listing of all the screenwriting contests get a copy of Narwhal Press's *Writer's Aide.* They keep track of all the writing contests around the country and constantly update their contest listings. The contests change often so they constantly update the book and run a new master. That means if you order the book today, you'll have the most recent contest changes.

The directory also includes entry forms for most of the contests and offers tips for entering, competitions to avoid, those that have been discontinued, and other helpful advice to the aspiring winner. The cost of the book is $25. That includes the shipping and tax. Add four dollars to that price for foreign orders.

In addition to publishing the *Writer's Aide,* the company publishes a quarterly newsletter. Here you'll find feature articles by script analysts and screenwriters. The newsletter is $20 per year.

To get one of the books or a subscription to the newsletter write, e-mail or call:

- The Writer's Aide, 1629 Meeting Street, Charleston, SC 29405; Tel. (843) 853-0510; Web site: *www.shipwrecks.com*. (You can also reach them via *www.hollywoodnetwork.com*.)

Following are the contests that offer the biggest pay-outs, either in money or contacts into the business.

If the contest isn't one of the well-established, recognized competitions, research it. Call or write the organizers and see if you feel comfortable that they are running a genuine competition that will be able to award the amount promised to the winners and/or provide connection with recognized Hollywood players. If the reward offered is a critical evaluation of your work, make sure the analysts are experienced in the business or at least in scriptwriting.

Following are the most prestigious and widely recognized competitions. Unless the big one hits L.A., you probably don't need to check their pedigrees.

- The Austin Film Festival and Heart of Film Screenwriting Conference
  Sponsored by: Festival/competition organization
  Entry fee: $35 per piece
  Prizes: Two winners each get $3,500; agency review of the script; work with an established screenwriter to refine material for commercial sale; airfare and pass to festival
  Contact: Austin Heart of Film Festival, 1600 Nueces, Austin, TX 78701; Tel. (800) 310-3378
- Disney Pictures and Television Fellowship Program
  Sponsored by: Film production company
  Entry fee: None
  Prizes: $33,000 one-year salary to develop your craft at Disney; all the advantages of working on the Disney lot
  Contact: Fellowship Program Director, The Walt Disney Studios, 500 S. Buena Vista Street, Burbank, CA 91521; Tel. (818) 560-6894
- The Nicholl Fellowships (Motion Picture Academy)
  Sponsored by: A foundation
  Entry fee: $30 per script
  Prizes: $25,000 paid in five installments over a year; this contest is so well-connected in the business that even the second-tier runners-up get noticed by agents and producers
  Comments: This is *the* contest in Los Angeles.

Contact: Nicholl Fellowships in Screenwriting, 8949 Wilshire Blvd., Beverly Hills, CA 90211; Tel. (310) 247-300; Web site: *www.oscars.com*
- The Sundance Institute
  Sponsored by: A film institute
  Entry fee: $25
  Prizes: Five-day writer's workshop twice during the year; Filmmakers Lab, a three-week workshop for writers and directors with advice from seasoned filmmakers
  Comments: This one is bigger and older than Nicholls. In fact, it's so well established that most of the entrants are advanced writers.
  Contact: Sundance Institute, 225 Santa Monica Blvd., Eighth Floor, Santa Monica, CA 90401; Tel. (310) 394-4662

The following contests are included because they offer prizes of $1,000 or more. Some are new; others are very established. As you go through you'll see which ones sound the most promising.
- The American Cinema Foundation Screenwriting Competition
  Sponsored by: A film foundation
  Entry fee: $30
  Prizes: $10,000 for winner; $5,000 to each of two runners-up; agents will read the winners' submitted work
  Contact: American Cinema Foundation, 9911 W. Pico Blvd., #510, Los Angeles, CA 90035; Tel. (310) 286-9420
- American Dreamer—Independent Filmworks, Inc.
  Sponsored by: Film production company
  Entry fees: $50, $75, depending on your submission date. The earlier, the cheaper
  Prize: $5,000 (for acquiring your script)
  Contact: American Dreamer—Independent Filmworks, Inc., P.O. Box 20457, Seattle, WA 98102; Tel. (206) 325-0451; Web site: *http://adfilmworks.com*
- America's Best/The Writer's Foundation
  Sponsored by: A foundation
  Entry fee: $35 for screenplays; $25 for TV scripts
  Prizes: $5,700 for each of two screenplay options; $850 for an original sitcom; $1,000 for an original TV drama
  Contact: The Writers Foundation, 3936 S. Semoran Blvd., #368, Orlando, FL 32822; Tel. (407) 894-9001

- Armageddon Films/Aspire Awards
  Sponsored by: A small independent film production company
  Entry fee: $25
  Prizes: First place: $3,500; Second place: $1,500; Third place: $1,000;
  possible option by Armageddon
  Contact: Armageddon Films/Aspire Awards, 34–17 Steinway Street,
  #915, Long Island City, NY 11101
- BlueCat Screenplay Competition
  Sponsored by: Screenwriting competition organization
  Entry fee: $20 for up to two screenplays
  Prize: $2,000 for first place
- Finalists listed in full-page announcement in the *Hollywood Reporter*
  Contact: BlueCat Screenplay Competition, 2633 Lincoln Blvd., #202,
  Santa Monica, CA 90405; Web site: *www.bluecatscreenplay.com*
- The Chesterfield Writers' Project
  Sponsored by: Film production company
  Entry fee: $39.50
  Prize: $20,000 for up to five writers, to participate in a year-long pro-
  gram with Kennedy-Marshall Productions and Disney Studios
  Contact: The Chesterfield Film Co. and Writers Film Project, 1158 26th
  Street, Box 544, Santa Monica, CA 90403; Tel. (213) 683-3977; Web
  site: *www.garlic.com/chesterfield*
- The CineStory Screenwriting Award
  Sponsored by: A screenwriters organization
  Entry fee: $35–$45 (depending on how late you are sending your
  entry)
  Prizes: $2,000 to each of three winners; software; subscriptions to
  screenwriting publications; travel and accommodations for the
  CineStory conference; meeting producers, et. al.
  Contact: CineStory Screenwriting Awards, The Monadnock Building,
  53 W. Jackson Blvd., #1005, Chicago, IL 60404; Tel. (800) 678-6796;
  e-mail: *cinestoryp@aol.com*
- Empire Productions Contest
  Sponsored by: Production company
  Entry fees: $30, $35, or $40, depending on the date of your entry.
  Prizes: $2,000 to winners in three categories; staged reading; public-
  ity for finalists; discounted attendance at L.A. writing conference
  Contact: Empire Screenplay Contest, 12358 Ventura Boulevard, #602,

Studio City, CA 91604-2508; Tel. (619) 276-1220; e-mail: *EmpireProd @aol.com*

- King Arthur Screenwriter Awards
  Sponsored by: An independent film production company
  Entry fee: $55
  Prize: $400,000 for each of the winners in three categories: action, drama, and comedy (paid over four years)
  Contact: Kingman Films, 801 N. Brand Blvd., #630, Glendale, CA 91203; Tel. (818) 548-3456; Web site: *www.kingmanfilms.com*
- Monterey County Film Commission Contest
  Sponsored by: Government film commission
  Entry fees: $40 and $50, depending on when you enter
  Prizes: $1,000 first prize; $500 second prize; $250 third prize; one-on-one consultation with jury member
  Contact: Monterey County Film Commission Screenwriting Competition, P.O. Box 111, Monterey, CA 93942-0111; Tel. (831) 646-0910; Web site: *http://tmx.com/mcfilm*
- The Nantucket Film Festival
  Sponsored by: A film festival/workshop organization
  Entry fee: $40
  Prize: $1,000
  Contact: The Nantucket Film Festival, P.O. Box 688, Princeton Street Station, New York, NY 10012; Tel. (212) 642-6339; Web site: *www. nantucketfilmfestival.org*
- The National Playwrights Conference
  Sponsored by: A writers organization
  Entry fee: $10
  Prizes: $1,000; month residency program
  Contact: The National Playwrights Conference, Eugene O'Neill Theater Center, 234 W. 44th Street, #901, New York, NY 10036; Tel. (212) 382-2790
- The New Century Writer Awards
  Sponsored by: A film festival organization and an independent film production company
  Entry fee: $25
  Prizes: $2,500 first place; $1,000 second place; $500 third place; reading of top screenplays by professional actors
  Contact: New Century Writer Awards, 43 B Driveway, Guildford, CT

06437; Tel. (203) 458-2900; e-mail: *omicronworld@snet.net*

- Script Connection Screenplay Contest
  Sponsored by: Writers organization
  Entry fee: $75
  Prizes: $2,000; $1,000; $500; submission to agencies; professional analysis
  Contact: The Script Connection, 10153½ Riverside Drive, Suite 389, Toluca Lake, CA 91602; Tel. (818) 623-7252; Web site: *http://home. pacbell.net/marion1*

- Slamdance International Film Festival
  Sponsored by: A studio-based film company and a Los Angeles literary/talent agency
  Entry fees: $45, $50, $60, depending on entry date
  Prizes: $2,000 first place; $1,000 second place; $500 third place; submissions to agencies/studios; software
  Contact: Slamdance Film Festival, 6381 Hollywood Blvd., #520, Los Angeles, CA 90028; Tel. (213) 466-1784; e-mail: *slamdance@earthlink. com*

- Taos Land & Film Company Screenplay Contest
  Sponsored by: A private real estate company
  Entry fees: $100 or $75 if a member of designated groups or a student
  Prizes: Five acres of land in Taos; one-year option on script for $2,000 to $50,000
  Contact: Taos Land and Film Co., 2554 Lincoln Blvd., #456, Venice, CA 90291; Tel. (310) 396-9242; e-mail: *Jeff@taoslandandfilm.com*

- Top Dog Productions
  Sponsored by: Small independent film production company
  Entry fee: From $30 to $60, depending on submission date
  Prizes: $3,000 first place; $1,500 second place; $500 third place; software; submissions to agencies and producers
  Contact: Top Dog Productions, 2567 E. Vermont Avenue, Phoenix, AZ 85016; Tel. (602) 840-6414; e-mail: *Topdogpro@aol.com*

- *Writer's Digest* Writing Competition
  Sponsored by: Writers magazine
  Entry fee: $10
  Prizes: $1,000 Grand prize, all categories (fiction, poetry, screenwriting); $500 to $25 for first through fifth place; $100 worth of *Writer's Digest* books for first through third place; sixth–eleventh place: *Writer's Market*

Contact: *Writer's Digest* Writing Competition, 1507 Dana Avenue, Cincinnati, OH 45207; Tel. (513) 531-2690; e-mail: *competition@fwpubs;* Web site: *www.writersdigest.com*

- The Writer's Network Screenplay and Fiction Competition
Sponsored by: Writers organization
Entry fee: $35
Prizes: $2,000 winners; $1,000 finalists; representation for two projects; professional writing assistance
Contact: The Writer's Network, 289 S. Robertson Blvd., Beverly Hills, CA 90211; Tel. (310) 275-0287; e-mail: *Fadeinmag@aol.com*

There are a few other contests whose prizes are not significant monetarily, but they are significant for other reasons. Most contests say they will get the winners' scripts to agents, producers, and analysts, but that can mean many things, including not much. If a contest is headquartered in Los Angeles or New York there's a better chance the winners will get access to top industry people. Again, however, check out the competition for yourself. These listings aren't an endorsement.

- The Christopher Columbus Discovery Program
Sponsored by: Carlos de Abreau, founder and chairman of the Hollywood Film Festival
Entry fee: $45
Prizes: Monthly winners: script notes, scripts shown to producers, agents; annual winner: $10,000 option, script sent to studios
Contact: Christopher Columbus Discovery Awards, 433 N. Camden Drive, #600, Beverly Hills, CA 90210; Tel. (310) 288-188?; Web site: *http://hollywoodnetwork.com*
- Shenandoah Playwright's Retreat
Sponsored by: Playwright's organization
Entry fee: None
Prize: For the one or two screenwriters chosen: three- to four-week paid retreat in the Shenandoah Valley during the month of August working on script and with other writers
Contact: Shenandoah Playwright's Retreat, Pennyroyal Farm, Route 5, Box 167-F, Staunton, VA 24401; Tel. (540) 248-1868; e-mail: *shenaarts @cfw.com*
- The Telluride IndieFest
Sponsored by: Festival organization run by Michael Carr

Entry fee: $40

Prizes: Staged readings; four nights free in a condo; ski passes for four days; discounts at local restaurants; passes to all festival events

Contact: Telluride Indie Fest, P.O. Box 860, Telluride, CO 81435; Tel. (970) 728-2629; Web site: *http://tellurideindiefest.com*; e-mail: *indiefest@ usa.net*

Not included here are contests that may offer prizes of $1,000 or more but are restricted in regard to setting, who can enter, and other such variables. To get a complete listing with entry forms, updates, and notes on each competition, get the *Writers Aide* and visit the contests' Web sites.

Good luck!

CHAPTER SIXTEEN

Holding On and Hanging In

Have you written three or four scripts by now and nothing's happened? Can't get an agent, and can't get your scripts to anyone?

You think you've done everything you're supposed to do. You've taken workshops or college scriptwriting and film classes. You've networked until you've felt like a switchboard. You've beaten your brains out for unique story ideas, you've had people you respect read your material and give you notes. Still nothing.

There are at least a couple of breakpoints along the path to success. There is a whole scale of people who talk about writing—from the lowest end, those people who tell you they will write one day to the highest on the scale, those who tell you they've written scripts but can't produce any evidence of it. You're past that point. You're also past the point at which writers, once they realize that they actually have to work at this career, give up and do something else, something offering a 401(k) plan and regular hours.

You face the next breakpoint. Success seems to elude you. You've decided that the power in charge of the universe harbors an ironic sense of humor. Noting that you want to succeed, the power laughs uproariously and spears you with all sorts of barriers. You conclude that if you can convince this power that what you really want to do is mow lawns for a living, then that goal will become impossible, but you'll finally get a break as a scriptwriter.

It doesn't help that every time you pick up *Variety* or the *Hollywood Reporter* you see some story of a writer, about fourteen years old or so, who just fell off an avocado truck, selling his first screenplay for about a zillion dollars.

Scenario two: You've had a little success. You've been asked to write some material for a spec sitcom, you've been one of the finalists for a game-show position, or you've gotten in to see an agent or two, but nothing has materialized yet. Still, it seems that the power is sitting out there in the universe somewhere chortling over your pitiful efforts to succeed at writing something to which you've dedicated a great deal of time while you're still working some lowly day job and watching your friends climb conventional ladders of success holding tightly to those 401(k)s.

Thank God for the parties you attend and the few people you know who are impressed that you're a *writer*. If you didn't get stroked by them once in awhile, you might never survive.

You're now asking yourself what you're doing with your life. This can be a superficial examination because you've already made up your mind to continue or to quit. Or this can entail real soul-searching.

While you're stewing through this pilgrim's progress, here are a couple of items to throw into the decision-making pot.

Learning to be a writer of screenplays doesn't necessarily come easy. Developing as a writer isn't like learning to be a good burger flipper at the local fast-food outlet. You have to be willing to keep on learning and keep on writing. You get better the more you write, which is why every successful writer will advise you to just keep doing it. Don't talk about doing it; do it. Most writers have a few manuscripts in their file drawers that no one has ever seen. They are the first efforts, the learning exercises. That may be what those scripts of yours are. Consider it training and keep on writing. Don't compare yourself to the exception that the trades profile.

Getting a script to the screen of your local movie theater is a complicated process that can fall apart at any of its various stages. Keep reminding yourself that the process is complicated. You haven't been singled out by fate to suffer exceptional difficulties. Unless you are born into the business or come equipped with exceptional contacts, challenges await your every thrust. Attitude's important. Some consider speaking to a pleasant agent's assistant a good day; others consider it a personal affront that the agent didn't take the call himself. You must see the glass as half full.

Rejection is as much a part of this business as celebrity divorces. If you have been writing for any length of time then you've read at least one story about an established writer suffering multiple rejections of a particular script before she made a sale—and she had a track record! You've read about writers who can't sell *anything* anymore even though they have proven themselves over and over. Why do you think you deserve smooth sailing? What makes you deserve to be exempt from these trials?

While you're wondering if fate has you singled out, step back for a moment and look at yourself. Imagine you are sitting in a shuttle cockpit watching the earth as you hurtle into space. The world looks mighty small and insignificant. Where do you and your problems fit in that picture? Read the Tao Te Ching or *Siddhartha* or First Thessalonians 5:16–18 to get some perspective.

Finally, you should stencil two words on your forehead: determination and perseverance. It takes heaping amounts of both to keep going until the studio calls with an offer you can't refuse, even longer before they call with an offer you can refuse.

In the meantime, above all, keep your good humor intact. You'll make it.

Index

Books from Allworth Press

Writing Scripts Hollywood Will Love
by Katherine Atwell Herbert (softcover, 6 × 9, 160 pages, $12.95)

The Screenwriter's Legal Guide, Second Edition
by Stephen F. Breimer (softcover, 6 × 9, 320 pages, $19.95)

Writing Television Comedy
by Jerry Rannow (softcover, 6 × 9, 224 pages, $14.95)

Writing for Interactive Media: The Complete Guide
by Jon Samsel & Darryl Wimberley (hardcover, 6 × 9, 320 pages, $19.95)

Writer's Legal Guide, Second Edition
by Tad Crawford and Tony Lyons (hardcover, 6 × 9, 320 pages, $19.95)

Technical Theater for Nontechnical People
by Drew Campbell (softcover, 6 × 9, 256 pages, $18.95)

Creating Your Own Monologue
by Glenn Alterman (softcover, 6 × 9, 192 pages, $14.95)

Promoting Your Acting Career
by Glen Alterman (softcover, 6 × 9, 224 pages, $18.95)

An Actor's Guide—Your First Year in Hollywood
by Michael Saint Nicholas (softcover, 6 × 9, 256 pages, $16.95)

**Writing.com: Creative Internet Strategies to Advance Your Writing
Career** *by Moira Anderson Allen* (softcover, 6 × 9, 288 pages, $19.95)

Marketing Strategies for Writers
by Michael Sedge (softcover, 6 × 9, 224 pages, $16.95)

The Internet Research Guide, Revised Edition
by Timothy K. Maloy (softcover, 6 × 9, 208 pages, $18.95)

Money Secrets of the Rich and Famous
by Michael Reynard (hardcover, 6½ × 9½, 256 pages, $24.95)

Please write to request our free catalog. To order by credit card, call 1-800-491-2808 or send a check or money order to Allworth Press, 10 East 23rd Street, Suite 210, New York, NY 10010. Include $5 for shipping and handling for the first book ordered and $1 for each additional book. Ten dollars plus $1 for each additional book if ordering from Canada. New York State residents must add sales tax.

To see our complete catalog on the World Wide Web, or to order online, you can find us at *www.allworth.com*.